THE MYSTIC SPIRAL

THE MYSTIC SPIRAL

Journey of the Soul

JILL PURCE

with 174 illustrations, 32 in colour

THAMES AND HUDSON

ART AND IMAGINATION
General Editor: Jill Purce
Drawings in text by Jill Purce

First published in Great Britain in 1974
Reprinted 1985

Printed in Yugoslavia

Contents

ACKNOWLEDGMENTS

Objects in the plates are reproduced by courtesy of the following:
Benaki Museum, Athens 42
Bharat Kala Bhavan, Banares 65
Biblioteca Apostolica Vaticana, Rome 48
Bibliothèque Nationale, Paris 34, 37
British Museum, London 7, 9, 10, 26, 27, 33, 45, 51, 52
Cairo Museum 18
High Commissioner for New Zealand 47
M. Hosokawa Collection, Tokyo 57
Minneapolis Institute of Arts 50
Museum für Islamische Kunst, Staatliche
Museen Preussischer Kulturbesitz 29
Museum of Fine Arts, Boston 19
Museum of Mankind, London 12
National Gallery, London 24
National Gallery of Scotland 36
National Monuments Branch, Dublin 56
National Museum of Antiquities of Scotland 46
National Museum of Ireland, Dublin 15
Öffentliche Kunstsammlung, Kunstmuseum, Basel 11
Palazzo dei Conservatori, Rome 22
Pierpont Morgan Library, New York 28
Private Collection 1, 14
Rijksmuseum van Oudheden, Leiden 2
Robinson and Watkins, London 35
Solomon R. Guggenheim Museum, New York 44
Tate Gallery, London 39
Trinity College Library, Dublin 53
Victoria and Albert Museum, London 4, 6, 20, 21, 54

Photographs are by the following:
A. J. Aldrich fig. 7
Alinari 23
Archives Photographiques, Paris fig. 77
Bildarchiv Foto Marburg fig. 36
Dr. E. M. Bruins 49
Peter Carmichael 59
Ciancimino Ltd., London 61
Peter Clayton fig. 55
J. E. Dayton fig. 45
M. Dixon 16
Professor Evans, University of London figs. 30, 55
Fievet 17
Fototeca Unione, Rome fig. 34
Ursula and Augusto Gansser 62
General Electric R and D Center fig. 69
Ian Graham fig. 75
Green Studio, Dublin 53
Sonia Halliday 60
Hirmer 13, 18, figs. 33, 59
Hunting Surveys Ltd., London fig. 97
Dr. Martin Hürlimann fig. 25
R. Lannoy 3
Andrew Lee 41
Mansell Collection 32
Leonard von Matt fig. 48
Edwin Smith 42
Eileen Tweedy 1, 4, 7, 9, 20, 21, 33, 54, figs. 19,
79, 85, 86, 91
Gregorio Vardanega 64
Roger Wood 8, 58

The spiral order running through nature and science, through mysti-cism and art, is the subject of an integrative book by the same author which is in course of preparation. The author would like to thank Professor Maurice Wilkins and Karlheinz Stockhausen for their help and encouragement, and the Leverhulme and Marsden Foundations for their generous support in the form of Research Fellowships during the period of the interdisciplinary project without which the present book would not have been possible.

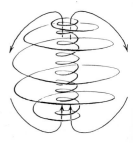

Journey of the Soul

In a second, the faintest perfume may send us plummeting to the roots of our being, our whole life verticalized by a fleeting sensation: we have been connected by a mere smell to another place and another time. The amount we have changed in the recognition of this moment – this is the spiral: the path we have followed to reach the same point on another winding.

All our experiences are like that haunting scent: situations recur with almost boring familiarity until we have mastered them in the light of the previous time round. The more we do this, the steeper the gradient, which is the measure of our growth. The spiral we travel round life is the means we have to compare ourselves with ourselves, and discover how much we have changed since we were last in the city, met our brother, or celebrated Christmas. Time itself is cyclic, and by the spiral of its returning seasons we review the progress and growth of our own understanding.

Ours is the spiral house we build to keep us from life's continuous outpouring, from an otherwise unchecked flow into the unknown. Since what is unknown has power over us, we should otherwise be as vulnerable as the snail would be if his shell grew long and straight. The familiarity of life's experiences curls round and protects us, creating those mysterious mountain views of half-concealed windings which keep us bright with speculation and anticipation.

The steepness of the straight path is prohibitive for most of us. The mystic calls this the 'short cut', the Path of Illumination; but that which lights the mystic's way blinds the ordinary man, unprepared for the light of full knowledge. For him, unveiled truth is death; instead he must make his gradual ascent, allowing himself the protecting reassurance of its gentle windings.

Flow, form and symbol

Like all existence on the descending scale of realities, the spiral is a symbol. It denotes eternity, since it may go on for ever. But because we necessarily conceive infinity in our own, and therefore finite, terms, we are forced to limit the limitless. It is only by imposing limits that we can make infinity accessible to us. Thus, in practice, the spiral will end; on paper, in two dimensions, we have in this space-time world to stop drawing it. The universe and man's consciousness (the macrocosm and the microcosm) consist in a continuum and a dynamic whole; this can be expressed by the spiral when, instead of ending, it is drawn either round a sphere or a doughnut ring, so that it joins up with itself by spiralling through its own middle. This symbol, which is perpetually turning in on itself, expanding and contracting, has an interchangeable centre and circumference, and has neither beginning nor end: it will be referred to here as the spherical vortex.

The perpetual inturning of the spherical vortex has analogies in nature with a stable form of flow created by the movement of air and water. This form, observed by blowing a smoke-ring or letting a drop of milk fall into water that has been allowed to settle, is called by scientists the vortex ring.

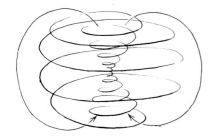 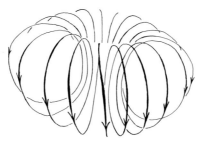 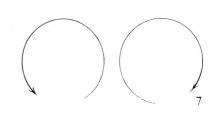

Within the totality of the universal continuum, we are limited by space-time to successive and analytic observations of its parts. These parts, the transient formations of nature's perpetual motion – although never perfect – seem to us to approximate to an ideal. In so far as the archetypal flow and growth form assumed by the mushroom, the embryo and the brain embody a forward impulse which turns back on itself, they demonstrate exactly the forming of a vortex ring.

Many formations in nature, although both constituted and caused by dissimilar phenomena, are not only similar to look at, but have identical mathematical descriptions. This would suggest that together they form a higher overall order outside that limited by our concept of linear cause and effect. The spiral movement which creates a centre and a 'whole' is also that which – combined with gravitational contraction – creates the solar systems, their suns and planets. The galaxies too are probably created by the inward spiralling of interstellar gas. These are the macrocosmic movements and cycles, mirrored in man the microcosm, which provide him with his model for all things cyclic, from sleep and emotions to time itself. The same vortical laws govern the movements of water, which composes nearly three-quarters of our physical bodies. Water is the pure, potential and unformed matrix from which all life takes its being. Consequently, the characteristics of its vortical flow, its ephemeral but changeless configurations, remain in all things as a testimony of their origin. It is from the involution of the unformed waters that the egg crystallizes by the turning in on itself of energy, of matter, or of consciousness; and all these are one and the same.

This order, reverberating down into the microscopic and subatomic levels, both structures and reflects our consciousness. The full significance of organization, which was obviously known to the Greeks since their word *kosmos* means 'order', is again being demonstrated by the physicists, who say that matter actually consists in its own movement and organization. Similarly, the growth of human consciousness is the continuous refining of its own organization, the ordering of its individual microcosm.

Although this process is built into the structure and is inherent in the natural evolution of man, it is one which can be facilitated and hastened with the aid of maps and guides. These maps are the mythological and religious systems which have been evolved by previous travellers, pioneers of the Way. Such a refining is alchemy, the transmutation of the natural man of the base metals into the spiritual man of pure gold, by repeated breaking down and building up (*solve et coagula*).

The following pages describe these maps and the ways in which man has understood the spiral of his own awareness. This spiral is not one, but many, which together constitute a spiral of multiple dimensions, in which each winding is also a complete spiral and each spiral just a winding. Furthermore, *we* are the spiral and all the spirals within. We need, above all, to become familiar with the nature of its movement, and consciously to make its laws our laws, like Edgar Allan Poe's sailor, who, by careful observation as he sank into the maelstrom, understood the nature of the vortex and was carried up by the spiral that had sucked him down.

The simple two-dimensional spiral has a number of remarkable properties. It both comes from and returns to its source; it is a continuum whose ends are opposite and yet the same; and it demonstrates the cycles of change within the continuum and the alternation of the polarities within each cycle. It embodies the principles of expansion and contraction, through changes in velocity, and the potential for simultaneous movement in either direction towards its two extremities. On the spherical vortex these extremities, the centre and periphery, flow into each other; essentially, they are interchangeable.

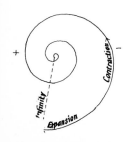

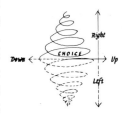

In the relative world – that of time, space and their corollary, motion – the potential of movement in either direction manifests as choice; hence, in three dimensions, the spiral may be imagined either as the aspiring upward spiral or as the downward vortex. The spiral is inherently asymmetrical, and any choice of direction along the vertical axis also determines a right- or left-handed path: the choice of travelling with or against the sun. That the latter, widdershins or 'sinister' direction has the associations it does is an indication of man's close relationship with the movement of the heavens: it is said to be the entropic, unwinding movement from order into chaos, or, according to C. G. Jung, away from the conscious and towards the unconscious. By virtue of this important asymmetry the spiral can be superimposed on its mate of opposite-handed-ness only by turning it through another spatial dimension: a flat spiral must be lifted out

of the page through three dimensions, or a spiral of three dimensions moved through four, and so on. Direction is thus an indication of the dimension, and in traditional thought the 'world', through which the spiral turns. Since our world is predominantly right-handed, the world above is thought to be 'left-handed', a passage through another dimension being implied. According to the Jewish mystical tradition, the Cabbala, there are four worlds, all of which exist negatively beyond their positive existence. Not until one is outside the relative world of space and time is there an end to the possibility of rotating an asymmetric figure through the next dimension in space to coincide with its reflection.

The universal spherical vortex is perhaps the most complete symbol by which we can map our cosmic journey. As William Blake wrote in his poem 'Milton':

> The nature of infinity is this: That everything has its
> Own vortex, and when once a traveller thro' Eternity
> Has pass'd that Vortex, he perceives it roll backward behind
> His path, into a globe itself unfolding like a sun. . . .
> Thus is the heaven a vortex pass'd already, and the earth
> A vortex not yet pass'd by the traveller thro' Eternity.

The evolutionary spiral

There are within every one of us three stages of knowledge. This is the spiral process by which not only individual man but the cosmos itself becomes realized; for it represents the course of evolution. Thus in the early days of humanity, as in childhood, there was no separation between ourselves and the outside world, until we, individually or as a race, became self-conscious. As a result of successive windings, our individual and collective ego crystallized, and we could see ourselves as subject, and as distinct from the world, which became the object of our scrutiny. As we looked, the continuum differentiated into 'things'. Each branched into more things, which in turn branched into even more, until the continuum had developed into a hierarchy; language, which once flowed in verbs and processes, broke up into nouns and connectives.

The third stage for the individual is that of intuitive knowledge or enlightenment, in which subject and object again become one. In collective terms, this return to a continuum implies not only the need for a new language, like that which physicists are trying to develop, but that the analytic and quantitative world is winding itself into a new simplicity. At the widest extent of the spherical vortex, the turn is long and slow before we are gathered up into the momentum of the contracting vortex of collective enlightenment. Each person who is integrated, realized and truly individualized becomes universal; and the extremity of differentiation of individual consciousness leads back into the Totality. In this spiral, every one of us all over the globe is like a light becoming gradually brighter, until there are so many and so intense, that there is one light, the light of cosmic consciousness, or what Teilhard de Chardin has called the 'psychical convergence of the universe upon itself': the Omega Point.

The breathing cosmos

Because any description of the Absolute must be limited, we are able to reveal it only by using symbols, which cut directly through all the layers and windings of our consciousness.

There is no space here to do more than touch on the profundity of these symbols; but they will be referred to throughout. Each is unity, either as the point or circle. Since a symbol cuts through all levels and therefore dimensions, they must also be visualized in three dimensions: each circle as a sphere.

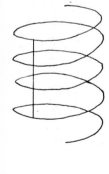

The function of symbolism is to go beyond the 'limitation of the fragment' and link the different 'parts' of the whole, or alternatively the worlds in which these parts manifest: these worlds are successive windings of the spiral. Each symbol is a link on the same frequency with the world above, a vertical bridge between objects within the same 'cosmic rhythm' on different planes of reality. In other words, each symbol links up with its 'correspondence' on the next spire. On a flat spiral, each point of intersection between a radius and the successive windings would be the successive manifestation of a symbol, traced through the respective worlds from the densest to the subtlest level of cosmic manifestation. We, like Plato's prisoners in the cave, can see merely the shadows of the images of the real objects, which themselves are only the manifestation of the Ideas and Archetypes (or Immutable Essences). In other words, even the 'originals', let alone the physical manifestations of nature, are but symbols of the metaphysical realities; and even these last, by virtue of their multiplicity, are but 'parts' of the One Essence.

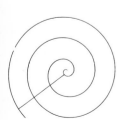

It follows, therefore, that all manifestation, or all that we experience, is symbolic, and that 'the whole of existence is a continuum which is ordered in itself. It has no manifest appearance and thus cannot be observed immediately by sense perceptions, but its inherent dynamism manifests in images whose structure participates in that of the continuum' (Wang-Fu Chih).

It is significant that, while the simple two-dimensional spiral is one of the most ancient symbols for eternity, it does not ever seem to have been a symbol for the Absolute. This is because it is not a *whole*; it can, by its very nature, never be complete. The implication here is that all our conceptions of the Absolute must be *more* than unlimited extension: they must *contain*. In all traditions God is seen as containing everything within himself. All manifestation extends from, and yet is contained within, the point, to which it also returns.

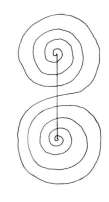

So, while the two-dimensional spiral starts in infinity and extends to infinity, passing through all the intermediary coils of manifestation in time and the relative world, it is only symbolic of the spherical vortex. This, one of the most ancient symbols known to man, is most familiar as the Yin Yang sign; and, although this was restricted to the Far East, the spherical vortex existed in the West possibly even earlier. Certainly it is found as the double spirals carved by Megalithic man.

Subject

When the flat double spiral is moved up into three dimensions, it has its origin and end in the opposite poles of a central axis: the central infinity, or axis of consciousness. The spiral has actually returned by winding *on* to its source. Its 'end' is not a second and therefore relativating infinity, as implied by the single spiral. The duplication of the One is simply *the One looking at itself, and in so doing becoming subject and object*: this is the duality by which all is known.

Object

Keeping this dual picture in mind, we now have a third element: *relation*. This distance between subject and object is knowledge; hence, in Japanese, the word meaning 'to understand' (*wakaru*) literally means 'to be divided'. On the Cabbalistic Tree of Life (fig. 40) this space is actually called Knowledge, or Daat, and is the invisible point on the central axis between the Crown (Kether), I AM, and Truth (Tepheret), I AM. It is understood as the link: *Eheieh asher Ehieh*: 'I AM [subject] that I AM [object].' This third principle is the mirror of consciousness by which pure Being looks at itself.

In the Islamic tradition it is said: '*I was a hidden treasure and I loved to be known, so I created the world.*' On the spherical vortex, the hidden treasure is the point of origin. In order for the One to be known – for there to be consciousness of the treasure *by* the treasure – the world was created. The cycles of becoming, the rounds of existence, spiral on and reveal their source by the creation of a vantage point: from its own opposite pole the source may view and hence be conscious of itself. The separation of heaven and earth gave the light of consciousness by which all is seen and known.

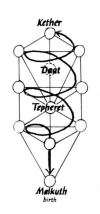

Kether

Daat

Tepheret

Malkuth
birth

This cyclic becoming appears in mythology as the protecting serpent or dragon which coils around the World Tree or Mountain – the central axis, the Axis Mundi. This dragon is also the world of illusion, the coils of manifestation, which the hero must destroy on his quest for truth, for the treasure, the incorruptible diamond of the Self at the still point in the midst of things.

This theme recurs in a more or less explicit form in most traditions: the world materializes and man spiritualizes along the same spiral. It is the breathing of the cosmos. With the exhalation the spirit contracts, creates, and *involves* or winds into matter; this is the creation of the world by the breath of God. With the inhalation, matter expands and *evolves* or unwinds into spirit. Man is the heart and microcosmic controller of this pulse. By becoming conscious he is inhaling – effecting the return breath.

We breathe in only to breathe out; this is true of the universe no less than of man, who was created in the same image. This is why the life of each person is conceived, in so many mystical, religious, and mythological systems, as the conscious unwinding of the original coils of manifestation.

Looked at on a single spiral, the path to consciousness has to be seen as a return along the same path; on the spherical vortex, the return is a continuation. At the point of maximum contraction, the expansion begins.

The alternating phases are described by the Cabbala. As each individual spirals down the Tree of Life, he involves into matter, being conceived in Daat and born in Malkuth or Kingdom; he thus brings heaven down to earth at the moment of birth, at which point the process is reversed, and through life he spirals back up the Tree, evolving or aspiring into spirit. He takes earth back to heaven, remembering in consciousness his original path. Indeed, all recognition, all knowledge of life, is a conscious remembering of the pre-conscious knowledge of the involving path.

The idea of unwinding was familiar to W. B. Yeats, who wrote:

> *Jaunting, journeying*
> *To his own dayspring*
> *He unpacks the loaded pern . . .*
> *Knowledge he shall unwind*
> *Through victories of the mind.*

Unwinding is the inhalation or expansion of the great breath. It is also the returning of the original impulse: the curling round on itself of the natural world, from the planetary orbits to the mushroom, from the recurrence of our experiences to the circulation of our subtle energies.

It is for this reason that conscious breathing plays such an important role in every form of meditation. Man is echoing the cosmic rhythms, the eternal creation and dissolution of the universe. This also accounts for the importance of the word and breath in so many cosmogenies, and, by extension, the idea of the creation of the world through the naming of things and the letters of the alphabet; this appears in the Cabbalistic, Arabic and Hindu traditions.

In Islam the breath is the 'Divine Exhalation', the manifestation of the Creative, the feminine principle of the One, analogous with the Hindu goddess Sakti. Manifested through this creative breath are the Divine Archetypes or names in the twenty-eight letters of the Arabic alphabet. The alternating breaths of 'continuous creation' are the origin of the Sufi ritual, the *dhikr*. This is the invocatory 'remembrance' of the original Divine act, in accordance with the saying of the Prophet: 'He who does not vibrate at the remembrance of the Friend, has no friend.' The pulsating breath and rhythmic invocation of the sacred Names culminates (as in the whirling of the Dervishes) in cosmic movements and vibrations of the whole body. With each outward breath the Divine Principle is manifest. It is returned 'back to the Divine Essence at every moment on the phase of contraction, and remanifest and externalized in that of expansion' (S. H. Nasr, *Three Muslim Sages*). Every moment of existence is thus integrated into its transcendent origin.

These alternating phases correspond to those of the waxing and waning moon; according to the Sufi mystic Ibn 'Arabi, her twenty-eight phases correspond to the letters of the Arabic alphabet, the forms of which are themselves traditionally derived from the lunar shapes. Moreover, since the letters are also phonetic, their form, sound and inner meaning as Divine names (or lines of force, or causes of the universe) are closely related.

The moon, whose cyclic rhythm we may not only watch by night but readily perceive through our emotions, has provided man with many associations for his awareness of the spiral, not least in its relationship to the rhythm and spiral flow of the water which constitutes the greater part of our physical bodies.

The life spiral

The spiral tendency within each one of us is the longing for and growth towards wholeness. Every whole is cyclic, and has a beginning, a middle and an end. It starts from a point, expands and differentiates, contracts and disappears into the point once more. Such a pattern is that of our lifetime, and may well be that of our universe. Only the time-scale has changed.

We begin our lives, as it were, a point: a tiny fertilized egg. In mathematics the point has location, but no dimension. Having no dimension, it is total possibility, and since it may expand equally in all directions, it is necessarily the centre. When we magnify or 'expand' this point, we find that our fertilized egg has become a sphere. Our goal is to return to the sphere: the sphere of psychic wholeness. If we have a goal to which we return, we have already presumed the path of life as the *time* between the point of total possibility, the germ bursting with the potential of our whole life cycle, and our physical death as a rounded, conscious entity.

If life is a path 'through' time, and therefore a continuum, we may also imagine it as a line; and further, since it returns and yet flows on, it is a spiral. Only if it were possible to come back to the *same point in time* could it be a circle. Any circular movement carried into the fourth dimension (of space-time) becomes a spiral; which is why apparently cyclic processes in time never repeat themselves. Even the earth's orbit round the sun is a spiral in time, and every year is different from the last.

Whether we impose the order of our perceptions on the apparently 'outside' world, or the outside world imposes it on us, there is but one order, and this order runs throughout both microcosm and macrocosm. Thus it is possible to say that our consciousness is a sphere, that we appear to circumscribe it spirally, and that the sphere of our consciousness as a whole appears to have its own spiral path; this is the microcosmic analogy to the movement of our own globe spiralling round itself and round the sun.

The movement of the earth turning on its own axis is the movement which gives rise to the circle and the angles of an individual's astrological chart. This circular chart, or image of psychic wholeness, is a map of the heavens surrounding the particular place

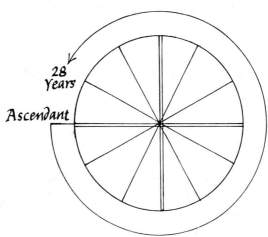

28 Years

Ascendant

on earth at the exact moment of birth. In a way we do not understand, the whole of each person's life-cycle is coloured by his birth event. The nature of this moment, the time and place of the first breath, is like the programme fed into the cosmic computer, while the permutating spirals of the celestial bodies are the composite parts or circuits of this computer, which all relate to and develop this single moment on the time scale of the individual.

Each of our inner faculties and modes of being is represented by a celestial body, and qualified by the natal position of that body; it thus has its own natural cycle of unfoldment while interacting with all the others.

In one lifetime, in relation to the unfolding of his lunar cycle, man makes three entire revolutions as from the ascendant, which is the starting-point on the circle and the moment of birth, like the hand on our individual cosmic clock. Each winding is like a complete circuit of the self about the self. Its three cycles represent the successive unfolding of body, soul and spirit, thought in some traditions to be approximately twenty-eight-year periods. If one draws this circle of psychic wholeness and divides it into four, the basis of the twelve-fold astrological chart, then one complete circuit takes twenty-eight years and each quarter corresponds to one of the seven-year periods allotted to the 'ages of man' ruled by the successive planets. The total life cycle comes to eighty-four years, or one cycle of Uranus.

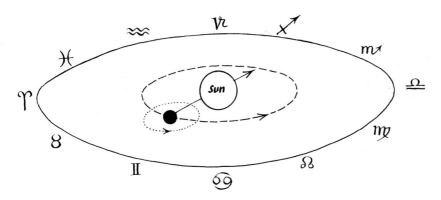

Although the earth moves round the sun, from man's viewpoint the sun moves round the earth, since, according to the monthly changes in the earth's position, the sun is seen against a background of the twelve different sectors of the earth's elliptical orbit which delineate the Zodiac. So the apparent movement of the sun through the constellations must be understood as that of the earth, and therefore of the individual person. This spiral of the sun (or of the earth's yearly movement) is that of our self relating to the outside world, while the spiral of our chart, revolving like the earth on its own axis, produces that of our inner being. The combinations of these two macrocosmic spirals in time, from our birth moment onwards, correspond to the main movements in the evolution of our consciousness.

In time, these cycles are spirals, whose symbolic direction, whether up or down, is the element of choice. As we learn to understand its nature, each spiral will metaphorically go up, since it is allowed to unfold. If we thwart it, it is repressed, and repressed energy is its own negativity. If its quality were fully understood, all the potential for development within each of us would be realized, and our path through the chart would spiral into the centre, the 'now' and the still axis around which we and the earth turn.

The two eternities

Situated between the poles, on our journey through the spherical vortex, we see at either end our source and goal. We are pulled in both directions, since the longing for the womb, described by some psychologists, has its counterpart in the passionate longing of the mystic for union with God.

For the first part of our lives we are predominantly outgoing, externalizing and developing our individual ego as a basis from which to cope with the world around us. This is the development of our first consciousness of self as a separate entity.

Starting from the pole, our initial windings are expanding. They start small, so that in the beginning it takes less time to complete one cycle. The relative speed of development and growth in a child, as seen from the outside, is prodigious in the beginning. Setting out as children, we have an enormous journey – our entire sphere to wind round – before we reach home once more. Each turn or cycle takes gradually longer to complete; objectively, the development gets slower, and the windings become gradually more stable as they approach the equator or turning-point. We can see the same development in two dimensions on the Yin Yang, where at the fullness of one cycle the seed of its opposite offsets the balance and causes a reversal of direction, after which, on the vortex as on all homeward journeys, the speed of rotation increases.

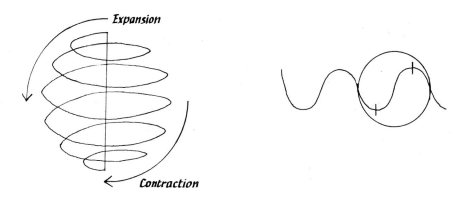

Each winding marks a containment and a completed cycle in the development of the whole; but, as each is a part of the whole, the completion is also a beginning, so that the spiral shows the enclosure and 'rounded' quality we experience, and the equivalent points reached at every new winding. The recurrent moments of crisis and decision, when understood, are growth junctures, points of initiation which mark a release or death from one state of being and a growth or birth into the next. 'How many times,' said Yeats, 'man lives and dies between his two eternities.'

Most traditions, mythologies, religions and legends describe these two eternities, the two ends of the life spiral. In psychological terms, for example, that from which we part with such reluctance is the undifferentiated matrix of the unconscious, an existence bathed in the pre-egoid memories of the watery abyss of our life within the womb. Everything here seems to have been easy and perfect, eternal and deathless; this was the Golden Age and Paradise, and that from which we were expelled.

The dawning of consciousness was a *self*-consciousness. By eating from the Tree of Knowledge we saw ourselves objectively – from outside and hence naked – for the first time. This was the first sign of our development, the turning round in order to observe ourself, and the consequent delineation of an identity and 'whole' within the unformed ebb and flow of unqualified bliss. This state is described in many of the creation myths, which are at once microcosmic and macrocosmic. The first phase in the ego's development appears mythologically as the cosmic egg. In the Hindu tradition it is the Golden Egg of Brahma (pls. 1, 65), floating on the waters of chaos: the first tentative separation, while still floating amid that which it contains and composes. Astrologically this is the · phase governed by the moon, for the moon controls the waters and reflects the sun, as the ego reflects the Self. The egg is formed by the inturning or involution of Being.

If the beginning of our journey was the Golden Egg or the Golden Age, its end is the rediscovery of that which we lost, the Golden Fleece or Alchemical Gold. But the right way back to the beginning is by going on. As the *Tao Te Ching* says:

> *Going on means going far,*
> *Going far means returning.*

To go back would be to go against the order of things, and to get sucked into the downward vortex. There can be a return to the centre only if there was first a departure from it, just as there can be no contraction without expansion. As one leads to the other, so the initial expansion and exploration of the developing being is checked by its return from unlimited dissipation into the infinite. Thus delineated, the 'ego' is contrasted with that which is outside the boundary, a God transcendent, and returns to dissolve its own delineation, to find God within and immanent.

The goal is at once a perfection of and a release from the self. Although these can be two distinct aims, it is also through the knowledge necessary for perfection that there is a release. The annihilation of the self in God, which is the Eastern goal of Nirvana, is also the release from the coils of Maya or illusion, the rounds of existence, and hence the passage from the spiral on to the central axis – the Centre in the midst of conditions – which is also the realization of the source in one's own being.

> *For what the centre brings*
> *Must obviously be*
> *That which remains to the end*
> *And was there from eternity.*

(Goethe, *Westöstlicher Diwan*)

On some paths the centre is dissolved; on others it has, by virtue of sheer perfection and knowledge, become transparent. In the Hindu tradition, the centre is called the 'Diamond Body' (figs. 67–69). This still point, free from the emotional turmoils of everyday existence, is described as something indestructible and unchangeable. In other traditions it is the Rock of Living Waters, the Ka'aba of the Heart, the Philosophers' Stone, the Stone of Sure Foundation, the pearl or jewel. The centre hardens, its transparency increasing, until, indestructible, it has the clarity of the diamond.

Seen on the flat spiral our journey can begin in infinity and move inward to the centre, the concentration of infinity into a point. Infinity is thus reached through a process of ordering and concentrating. The One which is everywhere can be found in the centre of being: a concentration of the One as everywhere into the One as centre.

This organization and concentration is implicit in the diamond, whose constituent carbon atoms, while the same as those of graphite and of coal, have here reached a state of maximum order and perfection. It is the clarity gained by such an ordering that is the goal.

The spiral journey which begins in transparency, at its most fluid in the unformed waters, comes to its final transparency in the perfection of the diamond.

The centre

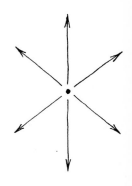

Since space is manifest it cannot be infinite. 'The point, which is the pivot of the norm, is the motionless centre of a circumference on the rim of which all contingencies, distinctions and individualities revolve' (Ch'uang Tzu). This point, being non-manifest, is total possibility, and contains – just as unity contains multiplicity – an infinite potentiality of manifestation, duration and extension. Since this potential extension is in all directions, the point is central. The universal spherical vortex can be seen as that which issues from the point, and contains it; it also conforms to the whole conception of the point as that which issues from itself and returns to itself, while still being nothing other than itself, which is yet All. In the same sense, in the Hindu conception, Bindu (the seed) is homologous with the world egg. It is said in the Hebrew tradition that 'the most Holy One created the world like an embryo. As the embryo grows from the navel, so God began to create the world by the navel, and from there it spread in all directions.'

In accordance with the fundamental principle of rotation which characterizes the physical universe, the embryo grows from the navel in a spiral. In the same way, time and the directions of space manifest from the central axis as the cycles of existence; thus the Dakota Indians say: 'The year is a circle around the world.'

Just as 'each part of the universe whether it be a world or a particular being is always and everywhere analogous to the whole', so 'every human individual . . . contains the possibility of making himself the centre in respect of the total being' (R. Guenon, *Symbolism of the Cross*). In their ritual, the Kwakiutl Indians chant: 'I am at the centre of the world.' Buddha says: 'It is I who am the peak of the world . . . it is I who am the Eldest.'

The centre is equally the centre of any place, or the centre of any person or being. In Greek philosophy, in the *Upanishads*, in the Cabbala and in Sufism, the centre within the human being is considered to be the heart, designated respectively the seat of Intelligence, of Brahma, of Solomon and of the Universal Logos. Although, physiologically, the heart is the centre of the circulation of vital fluid throughout the body, the heart in this higher sense is not confined to the corporeal state, and its location should not be exactly identified with that of its physical counterpart.

The Absolute, by becoming subject and object, divided itself into heaven and earth, thereby creating the Axis Mundi – the pole situated at the centre of the world, holding up the canopy of heaven and connecting it with the earth. It thus became the central axis connecting and penetrating the horizontal states of being, by passing through their centres, and 'the locus of manifestation of what the Far-Eastern tradition calls the actionless Activity of Heaven' (R. Guenon, *Symbolism of the Cross*).

It is pre-eminently man's function to act as the link between heaven and earth. Each person is therefore a central axis, and has within him a central axis, up which he must move or 'climb' by developing his various centres, or by activating the subtle energies within his spinal column, or metaphorically by climbing the central pillar of consciousness on the Tree of Life, which in turn effects the descent of light or grace from above. This descent, however, can only manifest when each person has realized, if only for a moment, the change of consciousness on to the central axis, the still point, or 'centre in the midst of conditions'.

This Axis Mundi, at the 'navel of the earth', takes the symbolic form of all pillars, poles, mountains, temples, spires or 'soul' ladders, and is the pole climbed by Siberian Shamans on their celestial flights, or that belonging to the Arunta of Australia, which, when found broken, caused the entire clan such consternation that 'they wandered about aimlessly for a time and finally lay down on the ground together and wailed for death to overtake them . . . denoting catastrophe, the end of the world, reversion to chaos' (M. Eliade, *The Sacred and the Profane*).

This axis breaks vertically through all the planes of existence, each of which is demarcated by a step or rung, whether the nine steps of the Egyptian Osirian Mysteries, the seven of the Persian Mithraic initiate, the seven steps of Buddha, the seven notches on the Siberian shamanic tree or the seven steps of the Babylonian ziggurat. Moreover, all cosmic or holy mountains, such as Meru, Gerizim, Kaf, Tabor and Olympus, constitute the primordial connection between heaven and earth.

The peak of the mountain is the tip of an upward spiral; it is the point of contact with heaven, which is an invisible downward spiral. Furthermore, all temples are replicas of the holy mountain: at Chartres cathedral one is told that the source of the well descends as far into the earth as the spires go into heaven, thus putting one at the centre. The spire constitutes the 'gate of heaven', or the opening in the upward direction, allowing direct vertical communication between heaven and earth.

From this axis, like the hub of the wheel, everything extends, radiates and rotates spirally. The entire universe, with all its spatial and temporal states, is but the spiral manifestation of the still centre; as it rotates it expands, and while still rotating it contracts and disappears to the source whence it came. Through meditation, man puts himself in the position of the whole, of which he is a symbol: his meditative activity simulates the activity of the whole. The *Tao Te Ching* instructs us:

> *Push on to the ultimate Emptiness,*
> *Guard unshakable Calmness,*
> *All the ten thousand things are moving and working*
> *[Yet] we can see [the void, whither they must] return.*
> *All things however they flourish*
> *Turn and go home to the root from which they sprang.*
> *This reversion to the root is called Calmness,*
> *It is recognition of Necessity,*
> *That which is called Unchanging.*
> *[Now] knowing the Unchanging means Enlightenment,*
> *Not knowing it means going blindly to disaster.*

God immanent or transcendent?

Mystical thinkers have always argued over the paradox: is God immanent or transcendent? Is the Absolute separated from us, the material world, by countless intervening spheres and planes, and perceptible to us only through emanations or manifested attributes? Or is this same Reality something implicit in the universe, in each one of us, in the Self at the heart of our being? Does, for example, our two-dimensional spiral begin in the centre and travel out stretching ever further towards God Transcendent, or is the direction of the journey inwards through the unfolding levels of awareness, until, as St Catherine of Genoa said, 'My me is God, nor do I know my Selfhood save in Him'?

Both halves of this dichotomy exist on the same spiral, whose *direction*, which is at once a *decision*, 'rests with the little arrow' (Paul Klee, *The Thinking Eye*). The potential of this spiral is simultaneous movement in either direction, and so a solution to the paradox.

By holding the centre of the spiral, and pulling it out of the page, we have in our hands, in three dimensions, the mountainous track, the central spiral along whose winding path so many wearisome ascents have been made. Each turn leads the pilgrim further from the world of illusion; each step in the ascent raises his Soul towards the Divine. Every step, however, not only takes him higher and therefore further from the material world, but it also leads him towards the centre, towards 'the divine essence dwelling at the apex of man's spirit' (Edith Schnapper, *The Inward Odyssey*).

Movement along this three-dimensional spiral is at once aspiring and centring, going towards God without and God within. Seen on the continuum of the spherical vortex, any journey away from the centre as the individual and the material world, and therefore towards God transcendent, leads at the same time on to the centre as the indwelling God.

We find this process depicted in diverse cultures and traditions, no matter at what stage in their development, as the spiral mandala, which is at the same time a spiral map of the soul's journey. Human consciousness is a microcosm; and so any diagram which initiates and directs its movement, as the mandala does, is acting as a map. The mandala has been called, by Giuseppe Tucci, 'the whole universe in its essential plan'. Any map of this cosmic journey, described in so many legends and mythologies, is also a map of consciousness and therefore a mandala. The spiral mandala shows the path through the universe, concentrating not on static perfection but on the equilibrium of its essential flow. Reality is not perfection except in the active equilibrium of the fusion of dynamic opposites. This equilibrium is the Yin Yang, whose interlocking spirals are a symbolic cross-section through the spherical vortex. The mandalic movement, described as the

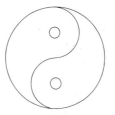

turning inwards through the centre of the outgoing energies, is the motion of the spherical vortex.

Thus, there are two approaches to the Divine, both spiral. One is an inward process of regeneration and integration, achieved with the aid of a mandala, and is a concentration into and through the centre; the other is the outward pilgrimage of Parsifal, Gilgamesh or Jason. The essential unity of the two is illustrated by the inward spiral of Bunyan's Pilgrim's Progress to the Celestial City, of Dante's climb to the summit of Mount Purgatory, and of Sudama's journey to the Golden City of Krishna.

Likewise, when this same paradox – God immanent or transcendent – is seen geometrically, in terms of centre and circumference, they are not simply interchangeable on the spherical vortex but spiral into one another. For all representations of the spheres, belts or layers of being through which man has to pass, depicted so often in the Middle Ages and Renaissance, are but abstractions of the spiral, since the time dimension must be accounted for. Thus the intellect, in its original sense as the spirit, may contain or be contained, be external or internal. As centre or circumference, it is the same. What changes is the viewpoint.

This change of viewpoint is so important in Sufi, Chinese and certain other philosophies that it is tempting to call it 'central to their outlook on life'; but the words themselves, involving a one-directional spatial metaphor, indicate that our language is ill-equipped to express a seeing on the spiral continuum of direction. Our language, governing the interpretations of our perceptions, works on the basis of measurement and division. Thus, the Sanskrit root *matr-*, to measure, is the source of the word for matter itself, as well as material, matrix, metre and Maya – the Indian concept of the illusion of measuring and dividing that we live by, and from which we must eventually free ourselves.

Microcosmic imitation of cosmic rhythms

The Chinese say that, just as the heavenly bodies have their celestial paths, so we have the Way, or Tao, which gives rise to all movement and is its law. The original form of the Chinese character 'Tao' means 'head'. It implies both consciousness and 'going', travelling a way. This would be 'to go consciously', or 'the conscious way'. Its meaning has been translated by Richard Wilhelm as the 'track which, though fixed in itself, leads from the beginning directly to the goal'. It represents the right way, the way of heaven, the way of man. The Tao is cyclic; we read in the *Tao Te Ching*:

> *There is a thing confusedly formed,*
> *Born before heaven and earth.*
> *Silent and void,*
> *It stands alone and does not change,*
> *Goes round and does not weary.*
> *It is capable of being the mother of the world.*
> *I know not its name*
> *So I style it 'the way'.*
> *I give it the makeshift name of 'the great'.*
> *Being great, it is further described as receding,*
> *Receding, it is described as far away,*
> *Being far away, it is described as turning back.*
> *Hence the way is great, heaven is great, earth is great;*
> *   and the King is also great.*
> *Within the realm there are four things that are great,*
> *   and the King counts as one.*
>
> *Man models himself on the earth,*
> *Earth on heaven,*
> *Heaven on the way,*
> *And the way on that which is naturally so.*

All the cyclic philosophies and concepts of time employed by man – the first of the five categories mentioned in the last four lines – model themselves in turn on the third – the movement of the heavens. Perhaps Taoism is the oldest of all. Its system, as laid down in the *I Ching* or *Book of Changes*, is based on a cycle of the sixty-four possible permutations of the two polar or opposing forces, Yin and Yang, in groups of six. Each of these groups of six, or hexagrams, is composed of two trigrams representing the union of heaven and earth.

There is a celestial model for this cyclic principle in the twenty-eight phases of the moon, where the polarity is found in the full moon and its disappearance fourteen days later. These phases form the foundation of Chinese astrology. The Hsiu, as the lunar mansions are called, are the circumpolar constellations which constitute the main divisions of the heavens. That there is a direct correspondence with Western astrology seems to be confirmed by the similarity between the glyph for Cancer, the only sign of the Zodiac to be ruled by the moon, and the Chinese Yin Yang symbol, which shows symbolically the whole system of spiral alternation and change. Like the Yin Yang symbol, Cancer has two opposing spirals showing the forces of expansion and contraction in dynamic equilibrium.

Yeats describes in his book *A Vision* a simple system of change based on these lunar phases, similar in its conception to Taoism. His cycle of twenty-eight is based not on the sixfold permutation of the polarities of Yin and Yang, but on the permutation of Objective (and primary) with Subjective (and antithetical). The comparison is striking when the circular chart of Yeats is compared with the cyclic sequence of hexagrams (see figs. 78–81). The degrees of change go from complete objectivity and passivity (Yin, North), through complete subjectivity (Yang, South), and on to complete objectivity.

All the concepts of Yeats, which are more or less veiled in his poetry, have their source in very ancient traditional knowledge. Although his system of change, based on the phases of the moon, is in principle Taoist and that of the *I Ching*, it nevertheless has its roots in the Western astrological tradition, which takes into account the natal moon phase.

Yeats's entire understanding of the universe was pervaded by the idea of opposing spirals, which he called 'gyres'. In their 'relative' state, the gyres appear as two spiralling cones. We read in *Ta Chuan*, the great treatise on the *I Ching*, an account of the antithetical spiralling trigrams (which can be visualized as the Yin Yang symbol). This account might equally be a commentary on Yeats's gyres, each of which he also saw as a triangle (or trigram) working in counter-phase with its opposite to form, when interlocked, a hexagram or six-pointed star:

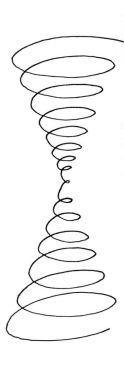

'When the Pa Kua (trigrams) intermingle, that is, when they are in motion, a double movement is observable: first the usual clockwise movement, cumulative and expanding as time goes on, and determining the events that are passing; second an opposite, backward movement, folding up and contracting as time goes on, through which the seeds of the future take form. To know this movement is to know the future. In figurative terms, if we know how a tree is contracted into a seed, we understand the future unfolding of the seed into a tree.'

Yeats's description (in *A Vision*) of the Absolute as the Thirteenth Spherical Gyre is none other than the spherical vortex:

'At any rate I can remember Robartes saying, in one of his paradoxical figurative moods, that he pictured reality as a great egg laid by the Phoenix, and that this egg turns inside out perpetually without breaking its shell.' (Although, in the original version, Yeats wrote 'a number of great eggs', he subsequently changed this to one, to symbolize the single thirteenth gyre or Absolute.)

In many of his meditational practices, man is consciously controlling and guiding the flow of the subtle energies within his body. Movement and life are synonymous, so that anything which prevents and obstructs it, by imposing rest and immobility, is the death principle. Consequently, Satan, whose name derives from Saturn, the astrological principle which constricts flow and movement, is conceived as opposing, since he prevents the unfolding of the One. For what no longer changes, or (since our language uses concepts of movement between states) 'turns' into something else, decays. Conversely, that which is kept turning, circulating, is the life principle. Meditation, whether it is vortex meditation, Kundalini Yoga, the ancient Chinese Circulation of Light as prescribed in *The Secret of the Golden Flower*, or the centroversion initiated by the contemplation of mandalas, is an analogy or imitation of – and therefore a participation in – the macrocosmic rhythms and movements.

Furthermore, the energy centres within the individual body themselves constitute microcosms; these are the chakras or lotuses. Each of them, in the process of developing consciousness, unfolds like a flower, spirally from within; all flower symbolism, particularly that of the rose, is an expression of growth and the unfolding spirit. Moreover, the Sanskrit word *chakra*, meaning 'wheel', indicates that the order and the law inherent in these centres is also that of all wheels, whereby the outside or periphery is kept in place and motion by radiating spokes from an inactive centre. This, related to the directional unfolding of the swastika in space and time, is the law implicit in the Wheel of Dharma – the sacred law of the teachings of Buddha. The Sanskrit metaphysical treatises, the *Upanishads*, say that, in order to follow such a law, it is necessary to turn the wheel within.

All images which prescribe these movements are essentially mandalic, centring and ordering, because, on whatever level, the movement is echoing the cosmic movement of which it is symbolic. All the spiral processes pertaining to the 'Great Work' of self-realization are but microcosmic analogies, reiterated within the body of man, of the universal vortical order.

The vortex sphere and the Tree of Life

The Tree of Life (fig. 40) represents, according to the ancient mystical tradition of the Cabbala, the successive emanations of the spirit of the One, vibrating 'upon the face of the waters' (Genesis 1), whereby the universe is created. The ten emanations (Sephiroth), with the invisible eleventh, Daat or Knowledge, and the relationships between them constituted by the twenty-two connecting paths which are the letters of the Hebrew alphabet (Divine attributes, like the Arabic or Sanskrit letters) constitute the model upon which everything, including all processes and particularly man as microcosm, is modelled.

Hebrew letters were also numbers, and their order is the order of creation. Just as in the Hindu tradition the Yogi must 'dissolve' creation by returning along its path in reverse and in consciousness, so the adept of the Cabbala must follow the spiral convolutions of the Serpent of Wisdom, 'rising in green coils from Malkuth to Kether'; for its windings follow, in reverse, the order of the letters, of the paths, and therefore of creation.

Even without a knowledge of Hebrew, we are told, the purest understanding of these paths comes from meditations on the shapes of the Hebrew letters, because, as was written in the Cabbalistic text, the *Sepher Yitzerah*, 'He drew them, hewed them, weighed them, interchanged them, and formed by their means the whole of creation, and everything that should be subsequently created'.

The universe, according to the Cabbala, becomes manifest through the materialization of four progressively denser worlds: Aziluth (Archetypal), Briah (Creative), Yetzirah (Formative), Assiah (Material). These worlds, which correspond to those of Plato, are depicted as superimposed trees (see fig. 93), in which the lowest Sephira, the Malkuth (kingdom) of each higher world, is the Kether (crown) of the world below.

There is always a change of direction between two successive worlds; the contracting vortex, spiralling down to the Malkuth of the Archetypal world, changes direction and starts to expand in its capacity as the Kether of the Creative world.

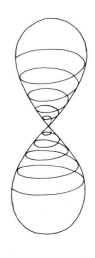

The life spiral of the individual may be understood in greater depth when it is superimposed on the Tree of Life. Every Sephira on the Tree has its planetary equivalent (fig. 40). The order up the Tree is that of the traditional 'Ages of Man' – the periods of life governed successively by the different planets. Astrologically, each life is an intricate complex of these permutating spirals and cycles; and each planet, with its successive 'sphere' of influence on the level of the individual life and psyche lasting approximately seven years, has its own speed related to its nature and what it corresponds to in us. Looking at the astrological correspondences on the Tree we find that the more refined faculties are the higher ones, and the ones whose planetary orbits take progressively longer. In other words, the more profound the cycle being developed, the more time is taken for its development, both on our vortex and in the cycles of the planets.

On the return path, the moon (Yesod on the Tree) is second to the 'moment of birth' at Malkuth and is related to the ego and the outward self or persona; it has the shortest cycle (monthly), and governs the externalizing, ego-developing phase of life, the first seven years, a subjective, fluid period of instincts and responses.

The sun (Tepheret) is the centre amid the orbiting planets. On the Tree the sun, which strictly speaking is in the earth's position, is the centre and essence of our being and has access to the higher faculties. The spiral path of our essential nature thus has the speed of the earth, and makes one revolution per year. At each birthday, it passes its point of origin.

Wisdom, associated on the Tree with the Sephira Hochma and the planet Uranus, takes a whole lifetime, or eighty-four years, to complete one cycle. The spirit, Kether, the Crown Sephira, or Neptune, completes only half a cycle within a single lifetime, and Pluto, which is thought to correspond with Daat, Knowledge, the invisible Sephira on the central axis, takes about three lifetimes to complete one cycle.

When the Tree is understood in terms of the relative distances and orbit-times of the planets, then, rather than going upwards through Daat to Binah, Hochma and Kether, the progression is up through Binah (Saturn), Hochma (Uranus), through Kether (Neptune) and finally back to Daat or Pluto. This is interesting because Pluto, observed closely by astrologers since its discovery, is thought to be the planet of regeneration, and therefore of initiation by death as descent and rebirth. (The god Pluto was king of the underworld.) By extension, Pluto has to do with all things like Daat, invisible. Furthermore, it is now thought to be the ruling planet of Scorpio, the zodiacal sign of the eighth astrological house, that of death and regeneration.

The Vortex-Tree, passing through Neptune at the crown and finishing in Daat, introduces a final downward spire that has a curious correspondence in the heavens with the uniquely eccentric path of Pluto. This path actually crosses the orbit of Neptune, as if it were the mediator between this world and the next. The cycle on the Tree ends, therefore, with a connection into the next world. Daat (Pluto), the point of death and rebirth, is one on the central axis with Malkuth, which corresponds both to the earth and the moment of birth.

The Vortex-Tree is only one winding on a spiral of a higher dimension. If the initial vortex is thought of as one lifetime, then this lifetime is one winding on a much greater cosmic evolution. Tradition has it that the evolution of the soul takes three lifetimes. After three windings on the spiral of the next dimension Pluto has completed one cycle.

If the Vortex-Tree is turned through ninety degrees, it bears a marked resemblance to the ancient glyph for the dragon, Serpentarius, which appeared on old maps of the heavens. This incorporated the male and female principles, Virgo, the spiral completed by the womb, and Scorpio, the spiral completed by the penis: embodying thereby the androgyne or 'complete man'. Discovered much later, the constellation Libra (between Virgo and Scorpio) brought about the separation of male and female. Thus, the astrological and symbolic goal is the balancing by the Scales of the two severed halves of man; the unity of the dynamic equilibrium symbolized by the completion of the Vortex-Tree.

Expanding and contracting spirals within the body

In the Hindu conception of creation, the transcendent One, Siva, who is the non-manifest point, the seed syllable OM, the germ Bindu bursting with latent creativity, unfolds as the windings of the feminine, Sakti, down through the successive cosmic vibrations and layers of being. It is the task of the Yogi to return in consciousness on the upward spiral, through all these layers, elements and sounds within his individual self. He is thereby completing the process in which Heaven, as manifested on earth, is realized or taken back to Heaven.

With the manifestation into grossest matter, the concentration at the apex of the descending gyre, the creative coilings of the feminine Sakti cease, and become latent within the body of each person, symbolized by the spirals of the serpent asleep with tail in mouth and her head blocking the entrance to the central channel. She is coiled $3\frac{1}{2}$ times round a vertical lingam, within the lowest of man's seven centres, the root chakra or fundamental support and pole of the body. Her name is 'Coiled', or Kundalini. She is Sakti, the creative energy or activity of the actionless God Siva, who is the point Bindu by virtue of which she exists, and around which she, as manifestation, revolves, like the coils of the dragon around the Axis Mundi or World Tree (see pl. 5).

In certain controlled meditations, it is the aim to awaken Kundalini, who normally sleeps while man is awake to the outside world, and to coil her up round the axis of the body, in order to fuse the pure creative cosmic energy with the inactive, pure consciousness of Siva (who takes the form of the unmanifest still point at the top of the head). To do this Kundalini, in the form of the subtle energy of the body, has to spiral upward round the Merudanda or 'axis staff', through the opposing spirals of the positive and negative or solar and lunar channels, Pingala and Ida, dissolving, as it were, her original creative coiling.

Conceptually, she is spiralling from the point Bindu out to the circumference, which she thereby creates; but because she is also spiralling back towards her union with the One, Siva, she is, while going outwards and unfolding, simultaneously going in

towards the centre, Siva, with whom she will ultimately fuse. This activity may therefore be conceived as a whole when seen on the spherical vortex.

Starting from the root and ending in the crown, her path is a return to the One from whom she issued. Since this yoga is considered essential for the prolonging of physical life, it is interesting to discover that, as Yeats wrote in *A Vision*, 'Alcemon, pupil of Pythagoras, thought that men die because they cannot join their beginning to their end.'

In the course of Kundalini's path, which may be straight up the central axis or spiralling, according to Gopi Krishna, 'zigzag through the spinal cord, exactly like the sinuous movement of a white serpent in rapid flight', her rising energy awakens each of the seven chakras. These lotuses, centres of energy at the root of the spine, the generative centre, the solar plexus, the heart, throat, third eye and crown of the head, roughly correspond in their positions with the various glands and plexuses controlling the different systems within the physical body. As Kundalini rises and pierces the successive chakras – each of which is itself a mandala spiralling around the central axis – the chakras unfold and transmute her energy into progressively finer vibrations. This is the reverse of the original process, whereby the vibration and sound of the oscillating three principles, or *gunas*, brought these levels into being as the gross elements.

At each level of development, with its corresponding chakra or lotus, the Yogi utters a different cosmic sound or mantric seed syllable. Each lotus has a different number of petals, each of which is a letter; together the petals constitute the fifty creative letters of the Sanskrit alphabet. Thus every sound and level of attainment on the aspiring path dissolves part of the original coils of manifestation. The rising, circulating energy sublimates through the elements in the reverse direction to its 'becoming', dissolving back through all the rounds of existence or manifestations of Sakti, into her original supreme union with the Absolute, Siva. This process, according to the Buddha, is the untying of all the knots in the inverse order to that in which they were tied, for 'he who knows the origin of things, knows also their dissolution'.

Man has always understood that his state of consciousness is related to the balancing and flow of his opposing subtle energy currents. These have been known in many forms and traditions. In the Cabbala, for example, the Tree of Life is also a representation of man, whose energy, the serpent of wisdom, must be activated and balanced within the opposing pillars. The Tree can thus be realized within everyone. The Caduceus, which is still used as a symbol of healing, is the rod carried by Mercury or the physician Aesculapius; its central staff (the neutral Sushumna in the Hindu tradition) is surrounded by the opposing spiralling serpents of the positive and negative energy currents. At the top are wings, symbolizing the 'winged radiance' of those who have achieved the dynamic equilibrium, the ecstatic union of these currents. These wings are also the two lobes of the medulla, the petals of the third-eye chakra, whose vision has been gained.

The opposing solar and lunar currents symbolized by the serpents are the alternating forces of expansion and contraction, manifested in the two halves of the Yin Yang symbol or the two halves of the double spiral or the world egg, and constituting, when joined, the spherical vortex. They are, furthermore, the two halves of the brain: the centrifugal, outward, differentiating principle, which corresponds to the right-hand side of the body, and the centripetal, unconscious life force, which corresponds to the left-hand side. The predominance of the differentiating, solar force blinds us to the unity behind phenomena, while by the lunar force we are bound to the eternal round of existence. Only a balance and union of these two may bring the light of pure consciousness.

The circulation of this 'light' or 'fire' is the basis of meditation in many forms and traditions. Therein, according to the old Chinese text, *The Secret of the Golden Flower*, lies the key to immortality. If these creative energies are not turned within, the body will be depleted of its life forces and dissipate unchecked into the outside world. This circulation is a conscious, backward-flowing movement, counteracting the normal outward flow and protecting the centre.

When the return, the principle of centroversion, has been effected, and when the centre which this circulation also protects has been reached, the gyration stops, just as the movement of a wheel becomes progressively less towards the still centre. Then the individual 'has reached the starting-point of all transformations, the neutral point at which there are no conflicts, and there he abides. By concentration of his nature, by nourishment of his vital spirit, by re-assembly of all his powers, he is united to the principle of all births. His nature being whole . . ., his vital spirit being intact, no one can harm him' (Ch'uang Tzu).

Another practice whereby the opposing energy spirals are controlled and turned within the body is vortex meditation, as taught to Yeats by MacGregor Mathers and his other spiritual teachers. Two conical spirals are visualized, whirling in opposite directions, one going up through the body and the other coming down to meet it. The two worlds, still distinct, are mirror images: the soul of man, the *materia prima* (below), reflects the universal spirit (above). The goal of the meditation is the union or inter-penetration of these two. Seen as Yeats so often conceived his gyres, they are two equilateral triangles apex to apex. The symbol here is that of the outstretched man, the hour-glass made up of the triangles of fire Δ and water ∇, of Yang and Yin.

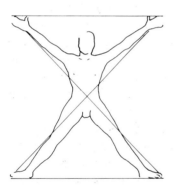

In the meditation, the lower vortex spirals up to meet and attract its spiritual counter-part. The mystical longing of man's soul for the spirit is here brought to fruition, so that the dualities of spirit and soul, of essence and substance, *forma* and *materia*, spirit and matter, *hsing* and *ming*, are fused in the 'conjunction' of conscious and unconscious in the heart. In the heart, the two interlocked gyres become the Seal of Solomon or six-pointed star, which in the Hindu tradition is the symbol of the heart chakra itself. The Cabbalists call this sixth centre the Seat of Solomon. Its name Tepheret means Truth and Beauty. Its position is that of the sun. At the centre of man and the Tree it connects and balances the upper and lower faces, while its paths extend like solar rays to all the Sephiroth around it. A similar conjunction may be seen in the extended diagram of the four successive worlds (figs. 93–94). When these interlock, the Malkuth of the first, Archetypal world is the Kether of the third, Formative world. In this way the entire second world of Creation lies between them. Likewise the whole Formative world lies between the Tepherets of the Creative and Material worlds. This means the heart, Tepheret, not only connects eight Sephiroth in one world, but also connects three of the four worlds.

When this contraction takes place on the Tree, the opposing vortices of the different worlds interlock, as they do within the body during vortex meditation, and create the Seal of Solomon. In the centre is the point, which here is both Daat (knowledge) and Yesod (foundation): the point of interchange where the knowledge of one world becomes the foundation of the world above.

Thus, symbolically, the two interlocking gyres of this meditation form the perfect man, Adam Kadmon. Alchemically the formula is *Quod superius sicut quod inferius*: 'As above so below'. Having six points, this symbol constitutes the union in man's heart of the six directions of space; it is the hexagram or union of heaven and earth.

These two gyres activated within man's body have their physical correspondence and are related to his two kinds of nourishment, his vibrational and physical food, which come from their heavenly and earthly sources and relate to the two opposing cavities in the body. In Taoist terms, the lower, larger, more expanded of these is the Yang cavity, relating to K'un (form) and containing the intestines, while the higher, more contracted or Yin cavity of the head relates to Ch'ien (energy), and contains the brain. Within these opposing cavities vibrational and physical food is assimilated spirally. Not only the processes and cavities, but also the openings through which the food passes, are complementary. Thus the mouth, which receives physical food, and the third or mind's eye, which takes in spiritual food, also constitute a pair, complementary and mutually exclusive in time, so that when one is active the other rests. Thus fasting is very important during periods of spiritual nourishment.

Each of the two bodily cavities has both an inner and an outer spiral. One outer spiral is the third eye depicted on royal headdresses, or as the spiral horn of the unicorn; the other is the umbilical cord through which we were nourished within the womb as we materialized into this world. The umbilical cord represents the contracting involution of our physical being: the means by which heaven is brought to earth. The third eye is the spiral of our spiritual expansion, the evolution of earth back to heaven; it is the means by which the Absolute is realized and made conscious.

When we gradually concentrate physically within the womb, this occurs through the umbilical cord, and subsequently through the intestines (the corresponding inner spiral). Our expansion and spiritualization takes place from the outer third eye and crown, and in the inner convolutions of the brain. Both the winding forms of the intestines and those of the brain have been depicted in religious and symbolic art as the labyrinth or spiral path, which creates, protects, and lays the *foundation* of the new town, temple or centre, and which opens to the man of *knowledge* and understanding; this is another example, therefore, of the Yesod/Daat exchange described above.

The 'invisible' third eye (the pineal gland thought by Descartes to be the junction of the divided body and soul) corresponds with Daat or knowledge, the invisible Sephira, and the planet Pluto; and the navel or solar plexus, centre of our contracting spiral, is analogous to Yesod or foundation, and to the moon. If knowledge of one world is the foundation of the next, then within the body, nourishment through the navel (Yesod) provides the earthly foundation for the spiritual knowledge entering through the third eye (Daat) from the world above.

Yeats saw this exchange in terms of evolution. Thus, his twenty-eight-phased lunar gyre lasts for two thousand years, after which there is a sudden reversal, point to base, base to point, and the commencement of the opposing gyre. Curiously, in his poem

'The Second Coming', at the 'death' of one gyre or age, the 'rough beast' that crawls its way to Bethlehem, to be born as the New Age, is symbolized by the unicorn with its third eye: the knowledge of one world moves, in its capacity as death and re-birth, into the next, and becomes the umbilical cord, Yesod, the foundation of the world above.

In the Christian Gnostic tradition, the Cross, a version of the Tree of Life, is called the Cross of Light. Light, synonymous with knowledge and consciousness, also consti-tuted the original manifestation of the Tree of Life, as the Tree of Lights, the seven-branched menora or candlestick.

'If the Saviour is enthroned as a messianic Lord, . . . it is because the community was waiting for . . . the return of him who dispenses the knowledge that delivers and who will thereby establish a supraterrestrial kingdom, a kingdom of Angels. It is not by shedding his blood that he saved the world . . . he is the Saviour because he has kindled for mankind the torch of perfect knowledge' (Henry Corbin, 'Divine Epiphany and Spiritual Birth in Ismailian Gnosis').

In the spiral of evolution, it is the function of the 'dying god' to pull the world up into the next winding of the spiral of a higher dimension. At the beginning of the Age of Pisces, Jesus on the Cross was the Saviour in this additional sense that he precipitated the exchange of worlds, which is also the change of 'Age' or the beginning of a new winding on the spiral of the next dimension.

The path of the redeemer on the Cross is thus the spiral path of the Serpent of Wisdom on the Tree. On the Vortex-Tree the moment of death – of knowledge and of rebirth – is Daat, through which mankind is pulled up (Pluto's orbit being the mediator between 'worlds') into the Yesod, foundation (or lunar position) of the next world. Thus it is that in the epiphanies of one Islamic sect, the Ismailites, 'the esoteric Church is drawn onward from cycle to cycle in a continuous ascending movement toward higher realms'. This is effected in Islam by the periodic cycles of the seven prophets. Each subsequent prophet draws 'toward him in an ascending movement the entire pleroma [spiritual universe] of his souls', 'succeeding the Angel who himself con-sequently rises into the celestial pleroma and from cycle to cycle continues to draw all those who follow him to ever higher abodes'. Each of the seven prophets is a concentra-tion, and a periodic culmination, an appearance of the True Prophet who, 'running through the ages since the beginning of the world, hastens to the place of his repose' (Corbin, op. cit.).

Each of the seven prophets symbolically pulls man – who is on his own individual spiral – up onto the next winding of a greater spiral, itself just one winding of a still greater spherical vortex. The spiral path through the Seven Pillars of Wisdom – the prophets – corresponds, therefore, to that through the seven-branched menora, the seven chakras, the seven planets and the seven days of creation.

Labyrinth and dance

The expanding spiral that creates and protects the centre, and the contracting spiral which dissolves it, are both concepts implicit in the labyrinth. By the existence of the labyrinth, the centre is created and protected. When the labyrinth is penetrated, the centre is dissolved. Entry and dissolution occur only under the right conditions: only with the knowledge of the way.

Although often intricate in form, the labyrinth is a spiral, and one which returns. It is a representation of the cosmos and all cosmoses, and hence of all ordered entities which correspond on the descending scale of analogy. It is therefore, at once the cosmos, the world, the individual life, the temple, the town, man, the womb – or intestines – of the Mother (earth), the convolutions of the brain, the consciousness, the heart, the pilgrimage, the journey, and the Way.

The earliest known labyrinth is that dating from the nineteenth century BC in Egypt; the most famous was in Minoan Crete. These, and some of the earliest spiral rock engravings from Palaeolithic times, are reminders of man's unceasing preoccupation with the spiral order and his own spiral development.

As the labyrinth creates and dissolves, expands and contracts, so it reveals and conceals. It is cosmos to those who know the way, and chaos to those who lose it. It is Ariadne's thread, whose windings create the world and yet enable us to unravel it – or ravel it:

> *I give you the end of the golden string,*
> *Only wind it into a ball,*
> *It will lead you in at Heaven's Gate*
> *Built in Jerusalem's wall.*

(William Blake, Jerusalem.)

This is the same thread that runs through the argument whose clue (the 'clew' or ball of thread) we follow; and, when we do not lose it, it leads us to the point. Yet it also conceals the point, disorientates us, and is the test of our endurance and knowledge.

The point or centre, in those labyrinths depicted in the pavement floors of many medieval cathedrals, is sometimes (as it originally was at Chartres) a depiction of Theseus and the Minotaur. The symbolism is that of the 'original' Cretan labyrinth – an initiatory hero test, the overcoming of death at the centre, and a subsequent return or rebirth into life, a regeneration on a higher winding. For, as it is necessary to be born from the womb to see this world, only he who is born from himself sees the other world. 'He who is not twice born will not ascend to the Kingdom of Heaven.' Other cathedral labyrinths depicted the architect at the centre, sometimes symbolized in the person of Daedalus, builder of the Cretan maze. Since treading the maze was a pilgrimage to Jerusalem in miniature, Daedalus also represents the Divine Architect.

In most labyrinths the spiral continues, and having reached the goal and centre, it either returns to the periphery and everyday life, or emerges on the other side, as it would on the vortex sphere of which this is a two-dimensional version.

In classical times, the labyrinth, together with its ritual circumambulation, was essential to the creation of a city. This ritual imitated or re-enacted the original cosmic creation; for when a space is set aside or delineated it is ordered, carved out from the surrounding chaos, and so sanctified.

Troia, or Troy, is still the name of many mazes – even those on English village greens. The spiral movement made chaos into cosmos, and protected the holy space thus formed from illicit entry. But according to the same law by which it both concealed and revealed, it also both protected and destroyed: hence, whereas the twice-yearly circuits of the Salii protected the city of Rome, it was seven circumambulations that razed Jericho to the ground.

The spiral or labyrinth, depicted in ancient tombs, implies a death and re-entry into the womb of the earth, necessary before the spirit can be reborn in the land of the dead. But death and rebirth also mean the continuous transformation and purification of the spirit throughout life; the alchemists use the word VITRIOL to stand for *Visita interiora terrae rectificando invenies occultum lapidem.* 'Visit the interior of the earth; through purification thou wilt find the hidden stone.' Such a descent into the underworld (the kingdom of Pluto) is the theme of most initiation rituals, and is comparable to the passage through the wilderness, or the 'dark night of the soul', which is experienced by mystics on their path. It is furthermore nearly always symbolized by the spiral. Those on the columns of the Treasury of Atreus (a relic of which is still to be found in the volutes of the Ionic column) have a further correspondence; by passing between two spiral columns, the initiate *becomes* the central axis or pillar of consciousness and equilibrium, for he has thus passed between the two opposite pillars of the Tree of Life, or between the coils of the serpents of the caduceus, and has thereby come into direct contact with the Source of Being.

The labyrinth governs (and also constitutes) man's circuitous windings through space and time, by ordering, guiding, checking and growing him both from and to his source. It is none other than a model of existence as we know it, a mandala, and a two-dimensional version of the spherical vortex.

However, the essence of the labyrinth is not its outward form, its delineating stones and hedges, but the movement it engenders. The spiral, mandalic movements of the dance predate even the labyrinth itself.

By dancing and emulating the macrocosmic creative dance of Siva, the whirling of the planets or the dance of atoms, man actively incorporates the creative vibrations and ordering movements of the cosmos. His body becomes the universe, his movements its movements, and when these are harmonious, then he is not only in harmony with himself, but with the universe which he has become.

In religious and mystical traditions, it is not only the God Siva who dances this incessant folding and unfolding of the world, of matter and its essence. This continuous creation and dissolution of matter and the world is the guiding thread which winds its way through the spirals of the Islamic arabesque and the spirals of their whirling dance. The Sufi mystics, the order of the Mevlana Dervishes founded by Jelladin Rumi, turn the manifest universe into being. By their whirling the Supreme Intellect is turned through all the spheres of existence down to the grossest matter.

In the Hindu and Cabbalistic traditions, the spirit rises by reversing the direction of the spiral through which the world manifests, and by expanding as matter contracts, as in the inhalation and exhalation of the spherical vortex. Similarly, by their progressive whirling ecstasy, the spirits of the Dervishes spiral up through the celestial orbits, which their movements represent, to union with the Divine. Their dance or 'turn' shows the successive degrees of manifestation into matter followed by those of the 'milling' away of their illusory existence, and the ascension of their spirits.

The first phase is that of the contraction; the Dervish starts his dance with his arms crossed over his breast, suggesting a junction in the heart of the descending and ascending vortices. He has his left foot firmly earthed, representing the still axis. By moving his right foot, he begins like a planet to turn on his own axis, while revolving with his fellows around a central sun, the leading Dervish. He gradually expands, uncrosses his arms, and, lowering his head over his right shoulder, he raises his right arm (of and in consciousness) to receive the Divine Emanation, and lowers his left to return his gift to the earth. He spins gradually faster, as if by his own revolutions he were connecting Heaven and earth by actually turning the spirit through himself and down into the ground, while his axis and heart remain absolutely still and his own spirit soars to its Divine Source. The greater his ecstasy, his expansion and speed, the wider his skirt extends. When his arms are both outstretched to Heaven, it is as if the union in his heart, delineated in its state of contraction (spirit into matter) by his crossed arms, has reached

its fullest expansion (matter into spirit) by the opposing gyres of arms and skirts: the outer expression of the bliss of the Divine Union in the very stillness of his heart.

For most of us, self-consciousness is still limited to the perception of our physical bodies, and even then, the greater part of our actions have become automatic. Certainly we have forgotten the depths of meaning behind the dance. Yet in spite of this, it is perhaps through the physical movement of our whole bodies that the spiral path may be most real to us. Every time we 'turn' or circle, in the movements for example of Scottish dancing, we are activating the inner energies and their cosmic counterparts.

We read in an early Christian Gnostic text, the Apocryphal Acts of St John, that Jesus led the Apostles in a hymn to the Father; its extraordinary rhythm and hypnotic quality vibrate through the words of St John:

> *And we all circled round him and responded to him: Amen. . . .*
> *The twelfth of the numbers paces the round aloft, Amen. . . .*
> *To each and all it is given to dance, Amen. . . .*

That this was an initiatory spiral, a progressive attainment of the Knowledge, is clear in the words of Jesus, who says: 'Even the passion that I revealed to thee and the others in the round dance, I would have it called a mystery.'

The winding upwards to the peak of full understanding is the seven-fold path of the Moslem round the Ka'aba, the goal of his pilgrimage to Mecca. The origin of the word *tāfa*, the Arabic name for this circumambulation, means 'to attain the summit of a thing by spiralling round it'. The centre, the square stone of the Ka'aba, is the 'Temple of the Heart' and the world axis. The windings are like the turning of the Buddhist Wheel of Dharma: the revolutions of the cosmos seen as the Immutable Divine Law.

Since the pilgrim spirals round the Ka'aba as the heart of the universe, it is also his own heart; and so the vortex being created is that of his own receptivity, which is matched by the descending vortex of Divine revelation.

Ibn 'Arabi in his *Meccan Revelations* describes his gradual ascent through the seven spheres of the Self – the heavens, planets or Divine attributes – until the Angel who accompanied him said suddenly:

'I am the seventh degree in my capacity to embrace the mysteries of becoming. . . .

'I am Knowledge, the Known and the Knower; I am Wisdom, the Wise man and his Wiseness.'

'Every cause is the effect of its own effect'

It has been man's tendency to forget, in his enthusiasm for objective knowledge, that, ultimately, subject and object are one, and merely opposite ends of the same axis. The consequence of this has been a swing back to a recognition of their identity, as expressed in the acknowledgment by the observational scientists of 'complementarity': light is both particle and wave, depending on the mode of one's participation in its being. In other words, the method of observation (that is, the nature of the observer) changes the apparently fundamental nature of light, and is not, therefore, totally distinct or apart from it.

The physicists are searching for a new language, not only to express this continuum, but also to express the cyclic nature of space and time. The understanding, for example, of the Sufi mystic Ibn 'Arabi, who says that 'every cause is the effect of its own effect', is of an order necessary for the physicists discussing the nature of matter, who say that, among strongly interacting sub-nuclear particles, each particle helps to generate every other particle, which in turn generates it. Like space, time is also curved. And indeed, in a science he has called *geometrodynamics* – 'the dynamics of the geometry of curved empty space' – one of our foremost cosmologists, J. A. Wheeler, describes how the very structure of our universe is none other than the vortex ring – a manifestation of the universal spherical vortex.

The sudden interest in the spiritual world, in the nature of the One, that has recently overtaken the West, is the violent redress of an imbalance. As all expansion leads to contraction, and out of every extreme is born the seed of its opposite, so our almost exclusively analytic and quantitative approach to the world leads into a new vision of the continuum; and we turn on to the next winding of the evolutionary spiral.

1 In Indian mythology the breathing cosmos is seen as alternating periods of activity and rest: the days and nights of Brahma. In an interval between successive creations, Vishnu reclines, having withdrawn the Universe into himself. He is seen within the Golden Egg in his threefold aspect: as himself, as the serpent Ananta-Sesha —who forms his bed—and as the Cosmic ocean upon which he and the serpent float. All creation is like a dream within him, ready, as he breathes out, to manifest from the potentiality of the primordial waters, as the spiralling of the cosmic serpent. (Gouache, Guler School, Indian, c. 1760.)

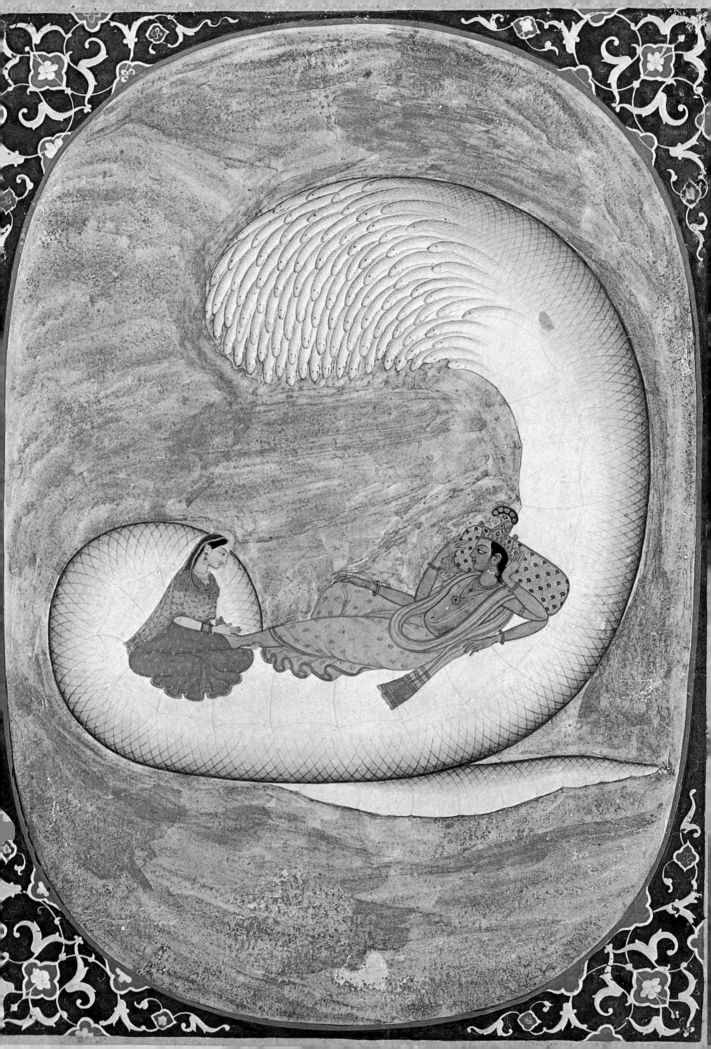

2 The 'Palace of the Intestines' symbolized and mirrored the universe at the moment of sacrifice. The omens and landscape described by the entrails were used by Mesopotamian diviners when founding a town. Space was thereby made sacred and chaos cosmosized. Representing the labyrinth, which creates order and protects the centre as it conditions entry, the intestines symbolized the convolutions of nature, the underworld and the 'unconscious', and the rite of passage whereby the neophyte is reborn into the state of knowledge and enlightenment. (Entrail-labyrinth, Mesopotamia.)

3 The great Serpent King of the underworld was one of the Nagas who embodied in Indian mythology the life energy, the powers of earth and waters. Guardians of the threshold, the snakes, like the labyrinth, coil round creating and protecting the 'treasure' at the centre, which is the sacred pearl of wisdom and divine knowledge. By harmonizing his natural energies, man can transmute these creative coils and endless rounds of existence to reach the axis and still centre of his being. (Carved cave ceiling at Badami, India, 6th century AD.)

4,5 After complaints from Indra, Vishnu devised a plan to preserve cosmic order. By insisting on the co-operation of the demons, his plan was to activate the dynamic equilibrium of the universal opposing spiral forces. Thus the demons and the gods alternately haul Sesha, the cosmic serpent, who is wound around the world axis, Mount Mandara, and thereby turn the central pole and churn the Milky Ocean to produce Amrita, the liquid of immortality. Within the body of man, this is the circulation of the subtle energies, visualized in the Hermetic, Cabbalistic and Tantric traditions as the serpent wound around the central axis, the serpent of wisdom or Kundalini. Often depicted as two opposing serpents, it is necessary to awaken and balance this energy as it winds through the active and passive channels of the spine or the active and passive columns of the Tree of Life (right); its Sephiroth (the heads) correspond to the different planets and faculties within man. By activating the central axis, the crown or goal may be reached, which is the timelessness and immortality of Perfect Man. (4 The Churning of the Sea Milk, painting, Punjab Hills, 19th century; 5 Illustration to Raymond Lull's *Opera Chemica*, 15th century.)

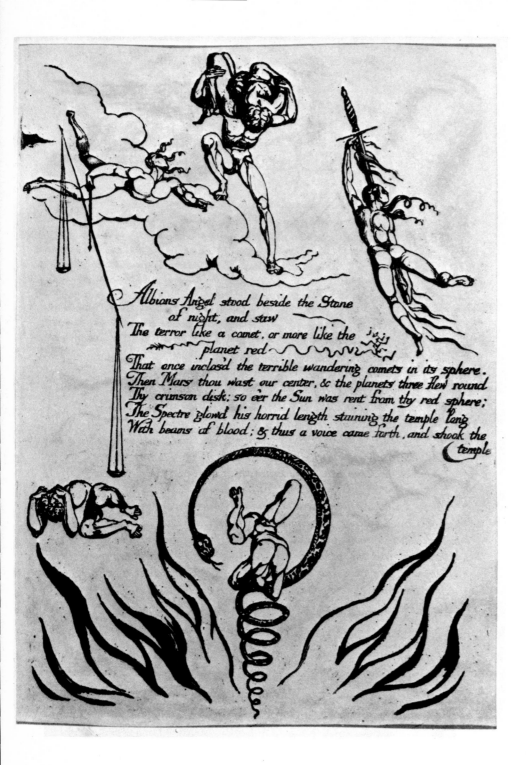

Albions Angel stood beside the Stone
    of night, and saw
The terror like a comet, or more like the
        planet red
That once inclos'd the terrible wandering comets in its sphere.
Then Mars thou wast our center, & the planets three flew round
Thy crimson disk; so e'er the Sun was rent from thy red sphere;
The Spectre glow'd his horrid length staining the temple long
With beams of blood; & thus a voice came forth, and shook the
        temple

6,7 The Tree of Life, or Knowledge (right), is the spiralling of the life energies in the body, shown here as two intertwining streams or forces. The serpent of wisdom (the saviour), whose energy this is, offers man the wisdom and self-knowledge that mastery of his own energy bestows. The world unfolds by the coiling of the serpent: he creates the central axis and thereby separates the One into two, into subject and object, good and evil and all the contraries by which man gains his understanding of things, and by which he may look back and be Selfconscious: no longer in the

subjective state of Eden. But, as Blake shows on the left, Maya, the differentiating world-view, permitted by dualism, may ensnare man in its coils of illusion: a spectre using reason without imagination, with a quantitative and materialistic perception of the universe. Unless the serpent power of polarity is balanced, it pulls man into the descending vortex. But, by a dynamic equilibrium of the two serpent forces within the body, he can attain unity enriched by multiplicity. (6 The falling spectres, from William Blake's *America, a Prophecy,* 1793; 7 Eve and the serpent, by Blake, 1796.)

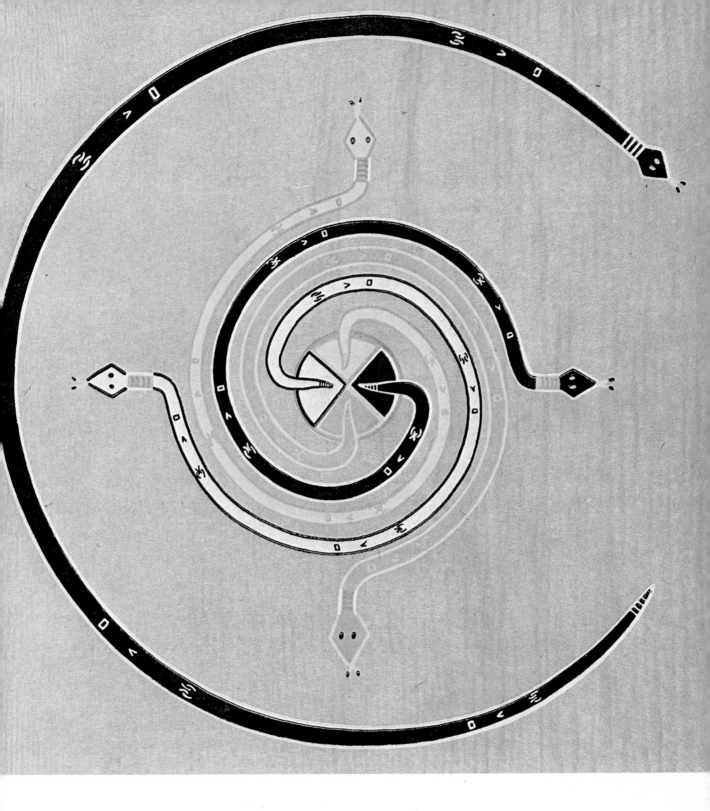

8,9 On the *khepresh*, the war helmet of the Egyptian pharaohs, the mastered serpent-force was seen at the third eye as the fire-spitting serpent, the Uraeus. This signifies the energy within the body is flowing freely and understanding has been gained. To initiate and control this state of flow is the real function of healing, or wholing, or making holy. The sand-painting mandalas of the Navajo Indians are for ritual healing. Every one is different and is applied to the condition of the person being healed, who might also be placed within it. As in all labyrinths, there is a circuitous path to the centre, here delineated by the opposing serpents, thought by the Navajo to be particularly powerful. The centre is a fourfold circle symbolizing the integration of the constituent parts of the psyche. (8 Prince Amun-Kher-Khopsh, tomb painting, Egypt, 20th Dynasty; 9 Navajo sand-painting from Gladys A. Reichard and F.J. Newcomb's *Sandpaintings of the Navajo Shooting Chant*.)

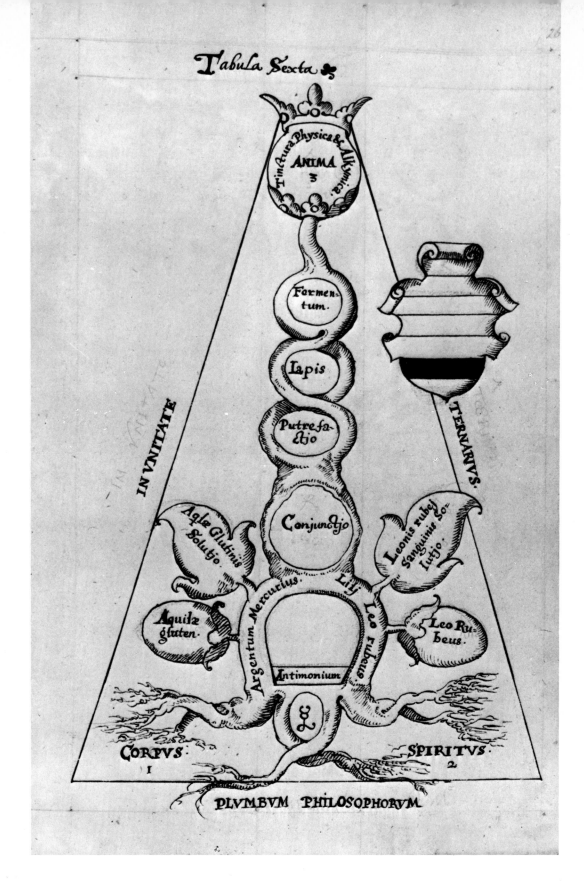

10,11 The evolution of the soul in the alchemical Great Work involves the unfolding of the two subtle energies, Sulphur and Quicksilver. In Hermeticism these two are termed Nature. Hence successively: 'Nature takes delight in Nature; Nature contains Nature; and Nature can overcome Nature.' The alchemist Nicolas Flamel, in his *On the Hieroglyphic Figures*, writes of Sulphur and Quicksilver: 'These are the two serpents which are fixed around the Caduceus, or Staff of Mercury, and by means of which Mercury wields his great power and

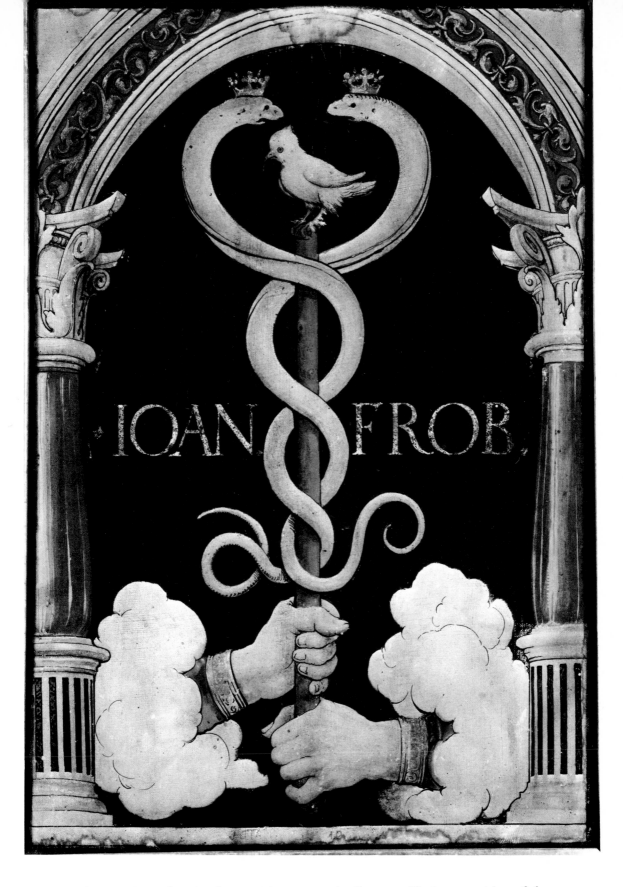

transforms as he will . . . so long as Nature remains "untamed", the opposition of the two forces is manifest in destructive and "poisonous" mode.' It was Mercury, by separating the serpents with his staff, who introduced the third equilibrating element. Holbein has crowned his serpents with the flames of wisdom, and balanced their power with the dove. In Matthew 10:16 Jesus says: 'Be ye therefore wise as serpents and harmless as doves.' (10 Illustration from George Ripley's *The Marrow of Alchemy*, 1676 edition; 11 Caduceus, by Holbein, 1523.)

12,13 'To seek the perfection of the warrior's spirit is the only task worthy of our manhood,' says the contemporary Mexican shaman Don Juan. 'The mood of a warrior calls for control over himself and at the same time it calls for abandoning himself.'
The balanced energy vortices on the body and head of this ancient Peruvian warrior are an outward sign of this state. In all traditions, and now in science, the left side of the body is passive: the Mochica figure holds his shield and kneels; Osiris holds his pastoral crook against the lunar left eye of the sky god Horus. This is the non-linear, 'unconscious', creative side (corresponding with the right hemisphere of the brain). The right side of the body is active and differentiating: the warrior's right foot is on the ground and his hand holds a club, alert and ready for action; Osiris holds a flail before the right eye of Horus. Osiris, god of the dead, guarding the threshold for the initiate, is thus balanced between the two eyes of the sky god; and, since his name means 'Seat of the Eye', he is the third eye. Symbol of fertility and order, of death of the old state and rebirth on to a higher winding of the spiral, he represents balance and enlightenment, the knowledge of the seer.
(12 Mochica warrior, clay, Peru, 4th–5th century AD; 13 Osiris, tomb painting, Thebes, Egypt, 20th Dynasty.)

14,15 Since death is birth into the spiritual world, the dying god is a symbol of knowledge, as is the cross or Tree of Life; and the Saviour is the Serpent of Wisdom. The cosmic forces seen here, permeating the body of Christ, are the same as the Hindu chakras or the Jewish 'shining ones', the Sephiroth on the Cabbalistic Tree (figs. 21, 40, 41), and their planetary counterparts. Rising to meet these centres (half right-handed and solar and half left-handed and lunar) are the vertical subtle channels. On his head is the flaming three-fold crown, the left-handed vortex of the descending spirit. Balanced by the four evangelists, Christ is at one with his fourfold nature and the four worlds. The earthly eyes of the Mexican figure are closed in the ecstasy of enlightenment, but his spiritual eye is open. In the form of the cross, both figures embody the state of balance between the horizontal, earthly principle, for which they are being sacrificed, and the vertical, spiritual principle. In this moment of knowledge they unify the six directions of space with the seventh, the still point at the centre around which all nature revolves. (14 'Laughing head' figure, Veracruz, Mexico, 6th–9th century; 15 Crucifix, gilt bronze, Irish, 7th century.)

16 Dying only to be reborn, Apollo, the sun, brings back light and the spring. Killing the dragon of darkness, he represents purification. Crowned by the golden spirals of his rays, he is, in the words of Hermes Trismegistus, 'set up in the midst and wears the cosmos in a wreath about him'. This Roman mosaic pavement, at once circular, spiral and fourfold, is, like many of the tiled labyrinths in medieval cathedrals, a mandala and picture of the universe. (Roman mosaic, detail, 1st century AD.)

17 Nowadays, auras are invisible to most people, but this was not so to our ancestors. The Eastern chakras, 'wheels' or vortical energy-centres of the subtle body are also called lotuses (the flower which corresponds symbolically to the rose). The south door of Chartres cathedral was opened to the knights, who were deemed to have reached a required level of spiritual under-standing; as they entered, their heads were at the height of Christ's feet. Through the door they would see Christ emblazoned against the brilliant spiral of radiating light: his halo, the rose window as a shimmering mandala. (Chartres Cathedral, south door and north rose window, 13th century.)

18 'In his upper member man has an image of God which shines there without pause' (Meister Eckhart). Increasingly since earlier periods in his evolution, man has lost the use, and consequent perception, of his supersensible organs—his force centres and energy currents. The vortical movement of this subtle energy was once familiar to him, however, as is demonstrated by its depiction in representations of countless heroes, gods and kings of early civilizations and tribal cultures. As well as by the serpent (pl. 8), worn here by King Senusret, the Egyptians showed the spiral of the third eye or radiant brow on the double crown of the Pharaohs. (King Senusret I and God Atum, relief, Egypt, 12th Dynasty.)

19 The old Chinese text, *The Secret of the Golden Flower*, tells us that between the sun and moon (the two eyes), 'there is a field one inch square which is the heavenly heart, the dwelling of light, the golden flower'. It is here, they say, that thoughts are collected, and light is circulated into a spiritual body. This light-body is the flaming pearl between two opposing dragon currents, the symbol of spiritual knowledge and enlightenment. (Crown, silver gilt, Liao Dynasty, China, 907–1125.)

21 The pearl being sought by the pilgrim Sudama is the Golden City of Krishna. Like the Buddhist Sudhana, he is the hero whose wanderings in search of the highest wisdom every devotee should emulate. The spiral nature of his quest for enlightenment, the circuitous route on which all such long and difficult journeys lead man, is echoed and affirmed by nature. Like the spiralling of the clouds and water, which enshrouds the Way of the dragons in mystery, the ambiguous forces of nature spiral into great vortices behind him; from their swirls strange natural beasts appear. (Sudama approaching the Golden City of Krishna, painting, Punjab Hills, India, *c.* 1785.)

20 For the Taoists, the dragon symbolized the Way, 'which revealed itself momentarily only to vanish in mystery'. Spiralling round in the clouds, the dragon, the spirit of changes, also dwells in pools, and like the Indian Nagas (pl. 3), guards great treasures in fabulous palaces at the bottom of the sea. Often comprising this treasure, and here being chased by one of the nine dragons, is the flaming pearl, symbol of the goal and spiritual perfection, of the mystic centre and divine wisdom. (Red lacquer vase, detail, China, mid 18th century.)

22,23 Joining man to heaven, the form of his hair describes the nature of his relationship with that celestial realm and the stages of his spiritual evolution. Within the temple of his body, man's head, the 'holy of holies', is the highest point, while his hair, its natural crown, is like the spire of a church, his vertical connection with God. Representing man's strength, it forms an antenna through which the spiritual force may descend. Of the three Gorgons, Medusa is the perversion of the spiritual and evolutive; thus she is crowned with the wild, chaotic snakes of un-

regenerate nature, subsequently overcome by Perseus, the hero and symbol of order. Buddha's curls, on the other hand, are the outward sign of his inner light and tranquillity. Chaos has been ordered, the serpent force mastered; the creative energy of Sakti has been married with the pure consciousness of Siva in the radiant unfolding of the thousand-petalled lotus.

(22 Head of Medusa, by Bernini, Italy, 17th century; 23 Head of Buddha, Tumchuq, India, c. 5th–6th century.)

24 St George and his fellow dragon-slayer St Michael represent spring and autumn, the yearly points of expansion and contraction, and thus mastery of the dual serpent force. They are twin aspects of Mercury, who brought harmony by taming the opposing serpents (pl. 11). Since both are associated with labyrinths and holy mountains, like Glastonbury Tor (pl. 41), their function is both interior and exterior. By seasonally piercing the dragon within the labyrinth (see fig. 57), they perform both acupuncture and geomancy: they tap, concentrate and disperse the subtle energies within the body and the geomantic forces within the earth (the Chinese 'dragon currents'). Emerging from the wilderness or the mystic 'dark night of the soul'—the forest, cave or labyrinth representing the unconscious and also the windings of illusion—the hero by the stroke of his lance achieves his goal, the princess who is his own completion. The cosmic nature of this moment, creating order within and without, is emphasized by the enormous spiralling cloud behind St George's head: what Don Juan (caption 12) calls 'reaffirmations from the outside world'. (St George and the Dragon, detail, by Uccello, Italy, 15th century.)

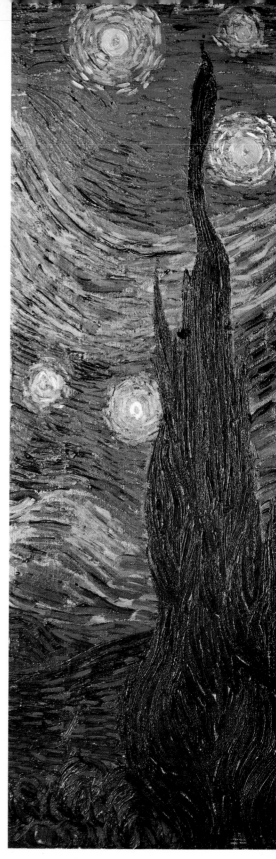

25 Another such affirmation is the swirling harmony between the forces of nature in Van Gogh's sky, where not only do the clouds spiral into the Yin Yang formation, but the opposing forces of sun and moon are unified. For Van Gogh this was a decisive moment of union between inner self and outside world. He wrote: 'First of all the twinkling stars vibrated, but remained motionless in space, then all the celestial globes were united into one series of movements. . . . Firmament and planets both disappeared, but the mighty breath which gives life to all things and in which all is bound up remained.' (Starry night, by Vincent Van Gogh, France, 1889.)

26,27 Leonardo's knot (above) is a mandala or contemplative diagram. It shows the manifold and complex web of the universe, which, like the labyrinth or the Islamic arabesque, is apparently baffling but made up of a single thread. When unravelled it leads us, like the thread of Ariadne, to the heart of our nature. The additional four diagonal knots, representing the four directions and the union of our own fourfold aspect, form a dynamic cross, symbolizing the ascending and descending vortices (as two triangles), the union of heaven and earth at the centre of our being. Also wound from a continuous thread is the mandala of Claude Mellan (left). Beneath is written: 'By the one the One is formed.' The spiral line, winding us to the centre at the tip of Christ's nose, not only recalls the unique capacity of the sense of smell to evoke past and future—or, at the centre, to verticalize time—but as the point of breath and inspiration it refers to the linguistic connection between spiral, inspire and spirit. (26 St Veronica's napkin, by Claude Mellan, engraving, France, 1649; 27 Concatenation, School of Leonardo de Vinci, engraving, Italy, *c.* 1510.)

28 Christ is seen crowning the Axis Mundi, the vertical connection with heaven, balanced by the horizontal, physical principle (pl. 15) and the coils of manifestation. This Tau cross, the Tree of Knowledge, shows the flow within the body, and its subtle energy centres, as a twofold axis and opposing spirals. The central spiral, the all-encompassing heart, expands like the ripples of the ocean to embrace the universe. (Initial Tau, Berthold Missal, Germany, early 13th century.)

29 The elephant is often known as the 'pillar of the universe'. His four-square stance, and the spiral of his ears, make him a symbol of cosmic orientation. Between opposing vortices (cf. pls. 11, 15), the crowning figure partakes in the cosmic life-fluid from which the original elephant emerged (pl. 4). (Elephant figurine, porcelain, Iran, 17th century.)

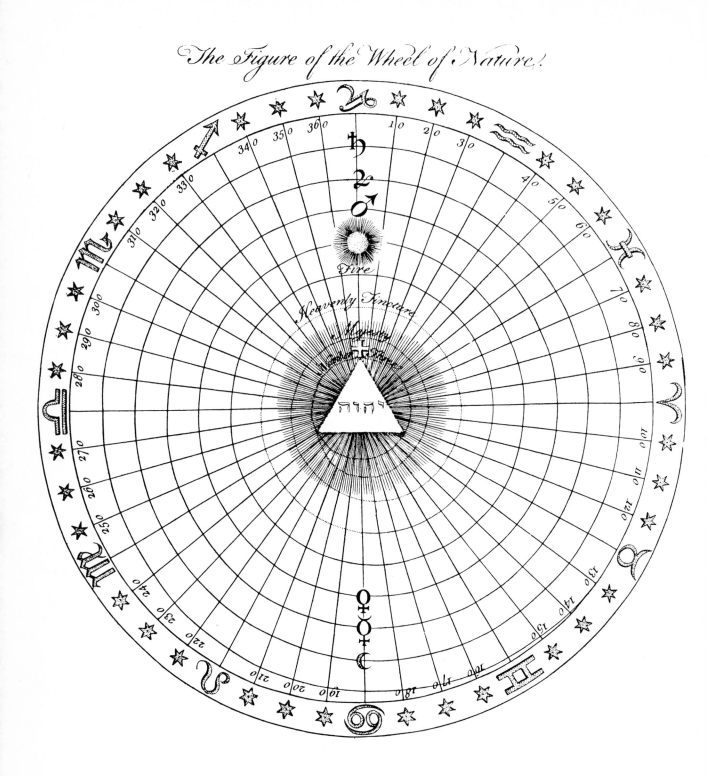

The Figure of the Wheel of Nature

30,31 Diagrams from two Renaissance mystics demonstrate the alternative conceptions of God, as immanent or transcendent. Boehme (left) depicts Jehovah at the centre of the spiral, of the cosmos and of man, while Fludd sees him as transcendent, separated from the earth by the twenty-two Hebrew letters or windings of the Cabbalistic Tree of Life. Fludd shows clearly that man's spiral path to God is the reverse of the original creative coiling which winds from the mind of God, through all the angelic hierarchies, celestial orbits and elements, down to earth, at the centre. While the straight path would be blinding, the position of the angelic

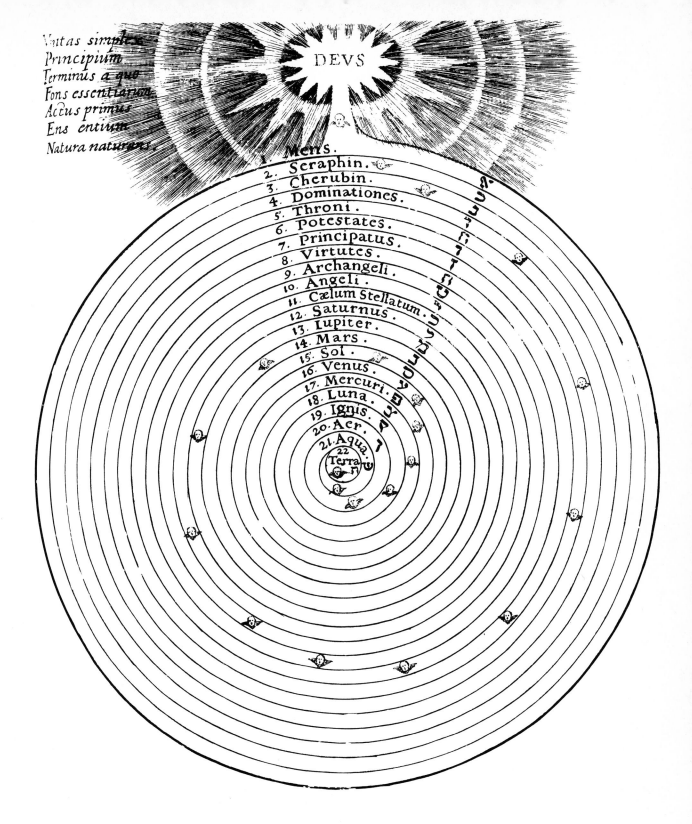

DEVS

Unitas simplex
Principium
Terminus a quo
Fons essentiarum
Actus primus
Ens entium
Natura naturans

Mens.
1. Seraphin.
2. Cherubin.
3. Dominationes.
4. Throni.
5. Potestates.
6. Principatus.
7. Virtutes.
8. Archangeli.
9. Angeli.
10. Cælum Stellatum.
11. Saturnus.
12. Iupiter.
13. Mars.
14. Sol.
15. Venus.
16. Mercuri.
17. Luna.
18. Ignis.
19. Aer.
20. Aqua.
21.
22. Terra.

heads suggests the possibility for man to accelerate the rate of growth of his spiritual evolution. Boehme, on the other hand, has depicted God in man's heart. Of his Wheel of Nature, both celestial and a picture of the mind of man, Boehme says that it 'windeth itself from without, inwards into itself; for the Deity dwelleth innermost in itself . . . even as God is everywhere Total and perfect, and dwelleth thus in himself'. (30 The Wheel of Nature, by the Rev. William Law, illustration to the Works of Jacob Boehme, vol. 2, 1763; 31 Diagram from Robert Fludd's *Utriusque cosmi . . . historia,* vol. 2, 1617.)

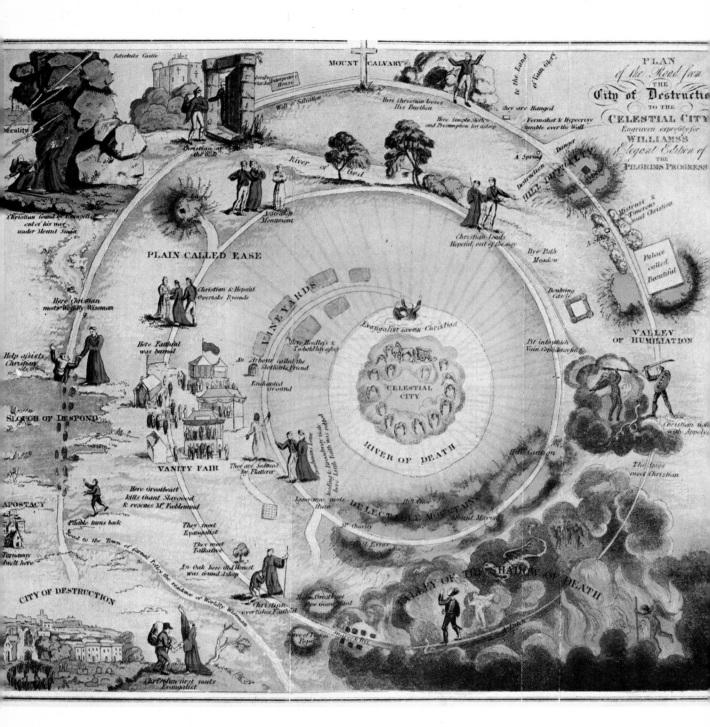

The labels visible in the illustration include:

PLAN of the Road from THE City of Destruction TO THE CELESTIAL CITY Engraven expressly for WILLIAMS'S Elegant Edition of THE PILGRIMS PROGRESS

MOUNT CALVARY

Beelzebubs Castle

Morality

Christian at the Gate

Here Christian loses His Burthen

Here Simple Sloth and Presumption lay asleep

to the Land of Vain Glory

they are Hanged

Formalist & Hypocrisy tumble over the Wall

A Spring

Danger Destruction

HILL DIFFICULTY

Mistrust & Timorous meet Christian

Palace called Beautiful

River of Life

Christian found by Evangelist cast out of his way under Mount Sinai

A Strange Monument

PLAIN CALLED EASE

VINEYARDS

Christian & Hopeful Overtake Byends

Here Headless & To behold lay asleep

Evangelist saves Christian

Pit into which Vain Confidence fell

Bye Path Meadow

Doubting Castle

VALLEY OF HUMILIATION

Here Christian meets Worldly Wiseman

Here Faithful was burned

An Arbour called the Slothfuls friend

Enchanted Ground

CELESTIAL CITY

RIVER OF DEATH

Christian fights with Apollyon

Help assists Christian

They are Soothed by Flatterer

DELECTABLE MOUNTAINS Mount Marvel

Hill Caution

The Spies meet Christian

SLOUGH OF DESPOND

VANITY FAIR

Ignorance meets then

Mr Charity

Hill Error

APOSTACY

Here Greatheart kills Giant Slaygood & rescues Mr Feeblemind

They meet Evangelist

They meet Talkative

Pliable turns back

Road to the Town of Carnal Policy the residence of Worldly Wiseman

An Oak here old honest was found asleep

Here Greatheart slew Giant Maul

PLAIN OF THE SHADOW OF DEATH

Turnaway dwelt here

CITY OF DESTRUCTION

Christian overtakes Faithful

Cave of Pagan Pope

Christian first meets Evangelist

---

32 The Pilgrim's Progress to the Celestial City is man's circuitous journey towards enlightenment, the spiral of unfolding consciousness in which similar situations recur on successive windings. As in all quests and journeys, symbolic of the windings of life, the hero is beset with trials. These, life's crises and tests, act as growth junctures in his evolution. (Illustration to John Bunyan's *The Pilgrim's Progress,* England, 19th-century edition.)

33 A 17th-century pupil of Boehme, Gichtel has placed the cosmic spiral or 'Wheel of Nature' (pl. 30) within the body of man, so that the celestial bodies relate to their corresponding energy centres (or chakras). He calls this man 'earthly' or unregenerate, since his spiral path, whose direction is yet uncertain, is still obstructed by the centres, which, like the dangers of Pilgrim's path, appear as the vices of human nature. (From J. G. Gichtel's *Theosophica Practica,* 1898 edition.)

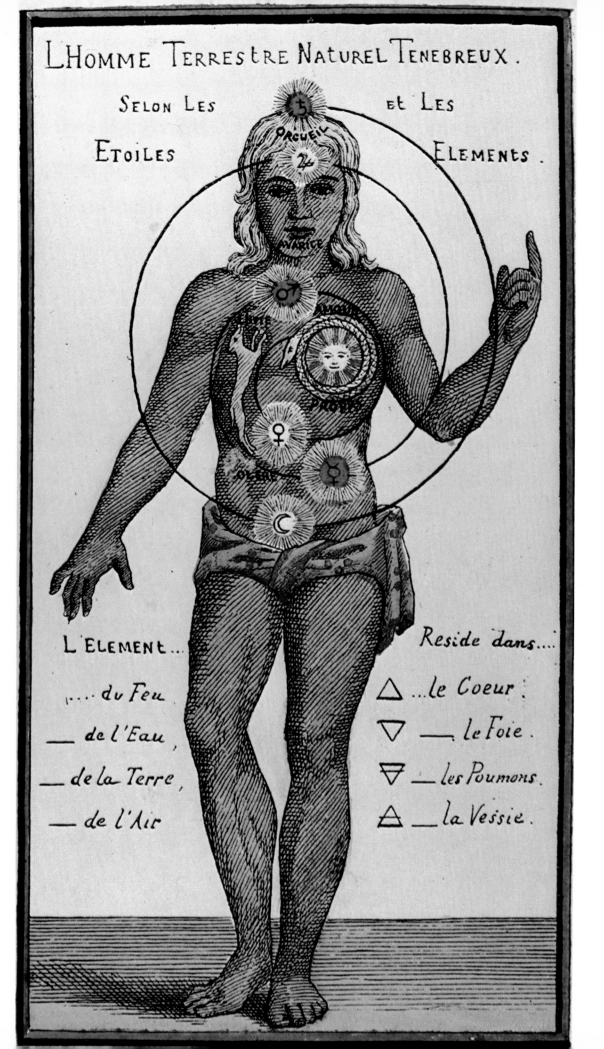

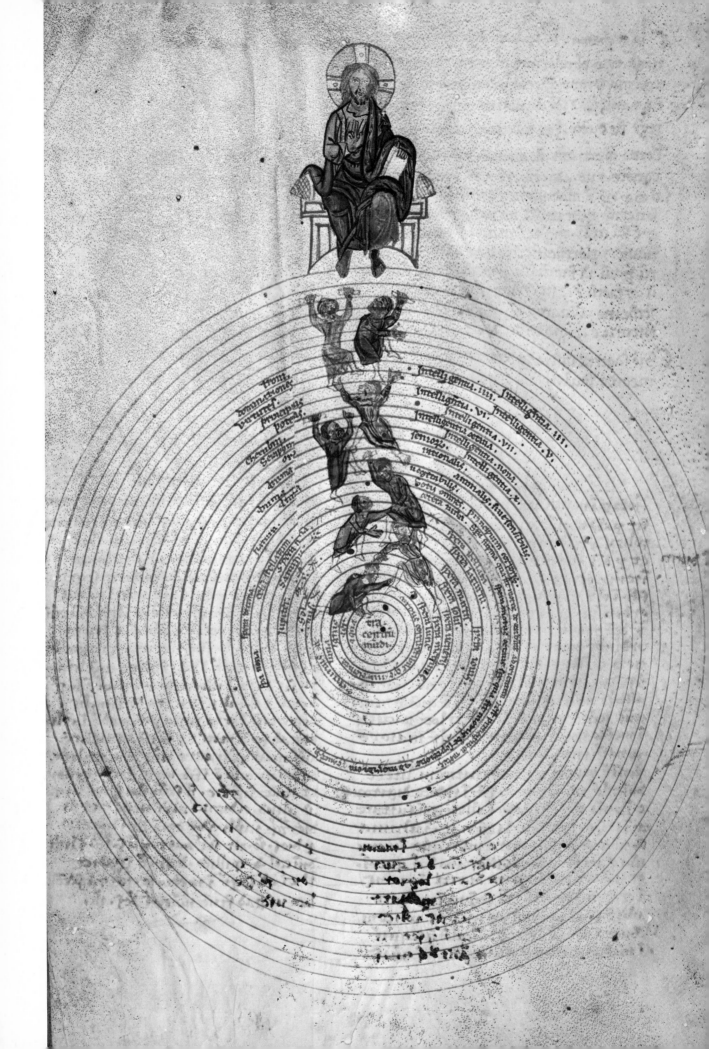

34 This Hermetic representation of the ascent of the soul through the celestial spheres may be understood as a macrocosmic counterpart of pl. 35, for both represent the interior evolution of man. The specific celestial spheres do not correspond, however, and are here seen as circles rather than the spirals of Boehme (pl. 30) and Fludd (pl. 31). The soul, or man, is shown clambering up from the earth using the celestial spheres as a ladder towards God transcendent. (Hermetic MS., Anon., 12th century.)

35 Rodney Collin thought that the energy centres and their corresponding glands were like adaptors and transformers. Like Gichtel (though their planetary correspondence differs), he lays these on an 'expanding spiral of function . . . the sun and source of which is the heart', ending in the pineal body as 'the ultimate outpost and possibility of the organism'. The functions have, in this development from the thymus gland, a gradation from the material to the spiritual. This corresponds, from a different viewpoint, to the spiral development through the Tree of Life according to the planetary orbits (figs. 41,43). (Man as microcosm, from Rodney Collin's *The Theory of Celestial Influence*, London, 1954.)

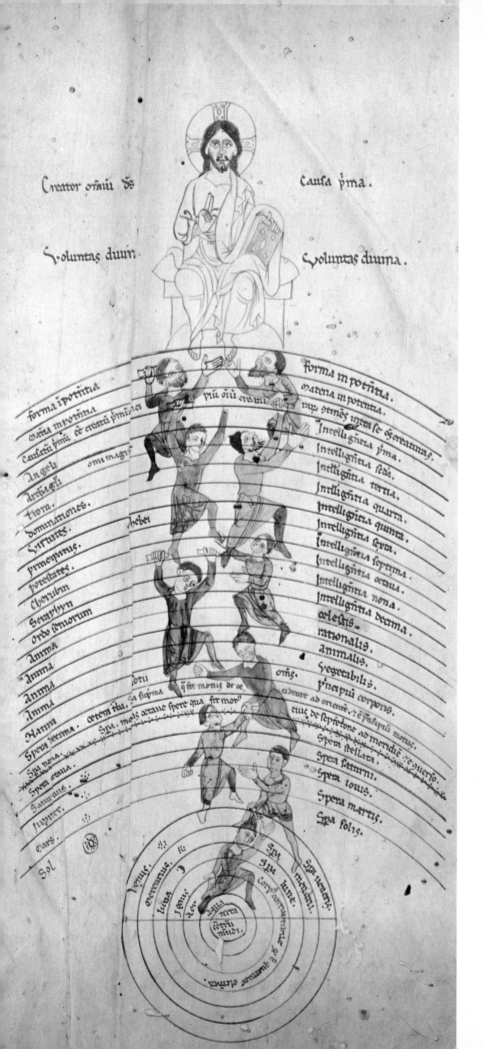

36,37 The windings of the spiral that sets Christ apart from the doctors (right) are traversed in the unfolding of consciousness towards the still centre of being. Like the maze, or the labyrinth of *Pilgrim's Progress* (pl. 32), they are the windings of life and the coils of the natural world around the world axis or unmoving spirit. At the centre of the spiral, Christ is immanent and within every one of us; he is also at the apex, and thus at the peak of the holy mountain (echoed by the labyrinthine hill outside), and therefore, at the same time, transcendent. In the Hermetic version (left), the soul spirals or climbs its way to God, enthroned above the world. Reversing the original process of creation, man passes through all the intervening spheres, the stages of gradual enlightenment. From the earth he travels through the four elements; the planetary orbits; the fixed stars; the principles of movement; the vegetable, animal, rational and celestial souls; the ten intellectual or cognitive faculties and their angelic counterparts; the First Created Being or Universal Spirit; pure potential form and material, and finally to God, the First Cause and Creator of all things. (36 Ascent of the soul through the spheres, Hermetic MS., Anon., 12th century; 37 Christ disputing with the doctors, detail, by Butinone, Italy, 15th century.)

38 The evolution of the spirit is an ascending spiral path to God. The tower of S. Ivo della Sapienza is made up of $3\frac{1}{2}$ windings (like those of the inner serpent Kundalini in Tantric teachings). These may be traversed, and are surmounted by a crown of fire, symbolic of the light which radiates from the enlightened, the masters of this force. Above this, for those having travelled the spiral path, is the orb or sphere surmounted by the cross, which together symbolize their inner state of wholeness or holiness. (Lantern of S. Ivo della Sapienza, by Francesco Borromini, Rome, 1642–60.)

39 Dante in his *Purgatorio* travels the same path, the spiral up Mount Purgatory (figs. 63,65), where his guide, Virgil, encourages him up the steep incline. Virgil is performing the role of Mercury (his own soul-guide) by leading Dante towards the wisdom which comes from the balance and reconciliation of all opposites, depicted in the case of Mercury by the serpents of the Caduceus. (Dante and Virgil ascending the mountain of Purgatory, by William Blake, watercolour, England, 1824–27.)

40, 41 Glastonbury (above), where Christianity – and some say Christ himself – arrived in Northern Europe, is a centre for the 'dragon currents' (caption 24), the terrestrial forces which connect the whole earth by a complicated network of energy flow. Glastonbury Tor is thought by some to be the Holy Grail and the goal sought by Gilgamesh and many heroes of old. The cup, it has been suggested, is the spiral labyrinth which encircles this cosmic power point. By delineating and concentrating the flow, such spirals create and protect terrestrial energy centres. Many, like this one, are associated with a form of the archetypal dragon-slayer who tames and taps its vortical energy. Even now, choosing a high peak surrounded by naturally spiralling ridges for his own spiral labyrinth, the artist may concentrate the natural energies of his site. Like the rock on the Isle of Skye, the hollow tower of St Michael makes the central vertical connection with the cosmos. (40 Stones on the Isle of Skye, Richard Long; 41 Glastonbury Tor, England.)

42 An early mandala depicting the orientation of Perfect Man. Owing to man's original clairvoyant faculties, and also to his knowledge of death and rebirth, the spiral was the symbol which unified the Neolithic world. This mandala combines the sacred numbers 9 and 7. In the early mystery religions, 9 was the number of Perfect Man, representing the stages passed by the soul on its way to birth, and thus also the return path to enlightenment. The central seven windings represent the six directions and the still centre. (Cycladic votive object, Greece, 2,800–2000 BC.)

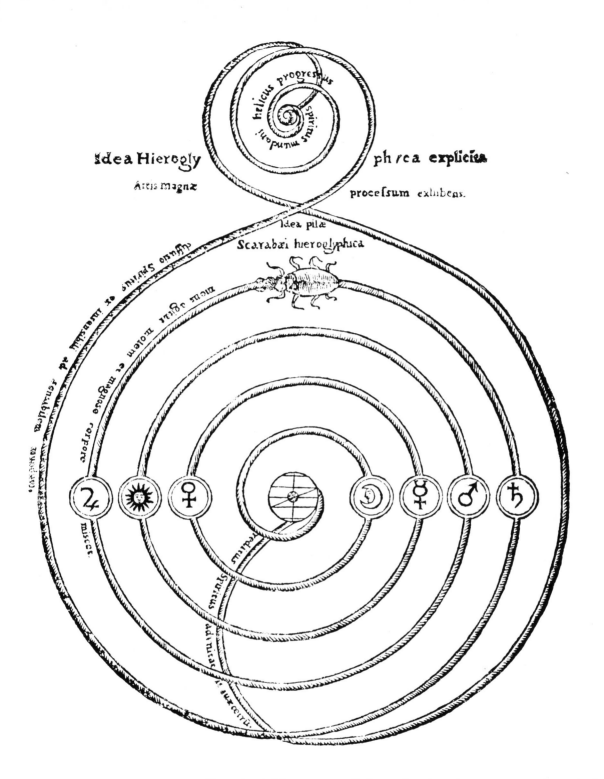

Idea Hierogly ph *rea* explica

helicus progressus

spiritus mundani

Artis magne   proce[sum exhibens.

Idea pile

Scarabei hieroglyphica

43 Egyptian initiates were called scarabs; these insects apparently push along their eggs, which contain their own regeneration. The path of this alchemist is a double spiral, representing the alchemists' alternate dissolution and coagulation, the expansion and contraction of the spherical vortex, and the phases of the subtle energies. 'The spiral progress of the mundane spirit' passes from his source through all the planetary spheres to arrive perfected at the centre; from there he expands, sees the centre from the 'outside', and spirals into the upper world, back to his divine source. (The key to alchemy according to the Egyptians, from Athanasius Kircher's *Oedipus Aegyptiacus*, Germany, 1652–54.)

44,45 Spiralling out of the crescent moon (Diana or Janus) is the seed of its immortality. The hare, nocturnal, prolific and traditionally lunar, is seen gambolling after it; as Blake also saw (right), the moon is the mirror or key to the door between this world and the next. The *Kanshitaki Upanishads* says: 'Those who verily depart from this world to the moon, in truth they go. . . . This verily is the door of the heavenly world.' Thus Jacob's ladder (Genesis 29:10–22) spirals through the moon to heaven. The ascending and descending angels show the spiral ascent of man's soul and the reciprocal descent of light or divine wisdom. Dying only to be reborn, and controlling nature and fertility by her cyclic rhythms, the moon is the seed of Jacob, promised by God to spread out in all direction: the spiral unfolding of the twelve tribes or zodiacal signs from Bethel, the central axis, the pillar of God's House. (44 The Hare, by Joan Mirò, Spain, 1927; 45 Jacob's ladder, by William Blake, England, *c.* 1800.)

46 'Peculiar stone balls', which were called Bethel or God's House by the Hebrews, were described, according to James Frazer, 'as round and black, as living or animated by a soul, as moving through the air and uttering oracles in a whistling voice which a wizard was able to interpret'. Every face has a different configuration of spirals and measures a span; almost a tetrahedron, it could be rolled like a die for divination. Found in association with labyrinth and passage graves, it may represent, like the Philosopher's Stone, the fourfold sphere of wholeness, the goal of death and rebirth. (Stone ball, from Glas Towie, Scotland, 3rd millennium B C.)

47 By inscribing on his own body what later man incised on stone, ancient man enhanced and controlled the energy flow that the vortices represented. It is thus that the spiral represents the key to immortality. Polynesian tradition recounts how the soul after death meets a dreadful hag, who, devouring his spiral tattoos, says 'Pass from Maura, land of the living, to Bouro, land of the dead.' Then, by touching the soul's eyes, she gives it the 'vision of the spirits'. If she finds no tattoos, she eats the eyeballs, blinding the soul and preventing it from finding immortality. (Head of a Maori, New Zealand.)

48 The negative vortex. Botticelli has shown a spiral cross-section
of the pit of Hell. Both hollow and downwards, it is the reverse
of the Holy Mountain symbolized opposite by the Minaret of
Samarra. It is, Dante says, 'to gain full experience of the Way He
comes; wherefore behoves him to be led ... Gyre after gyre
through Hell,' for eventually the contracting path changes to the
expansion of Mount Purgatory, and the soul's ascent. (Dante's
Inferno, illustration by Sandro Botticelli, Italy, 16th century.)

49 The spiral ascent of this holy mountain is symbolic of the
expansion and evolution of consciousness and the accompanying
flame of wisdom. As the pilgrim travels towards God, so his
receptivity is met by the descending spiral, the manifestation of
the spirit. Indeed, since minarets are used for launching prayers,
it is as if the spiral dynamic propels the word on vortices of air
towards the Divine. (Minaret of the Mosque of Samarra, Iraq,
9th century.)

50,51 To the Chinese the owl represents night, and to the Egyptians the dead sun on its nocturnal journey across the sea of darkness. It is the cold, passive, Yin and chaotic principle of the universe, which must be ordered, as symbolized by the spiral on the bird's breast. On the coin from Knossos, the spiral is replaced by the labyrinth (pl. 2), the bringer of order, and the device by which chaos is made into cosmos and space made sacred. (50 Wine vessel in the form of an owl, China, 1st millennium BC; 51 Coin from Knossos, Crete.)

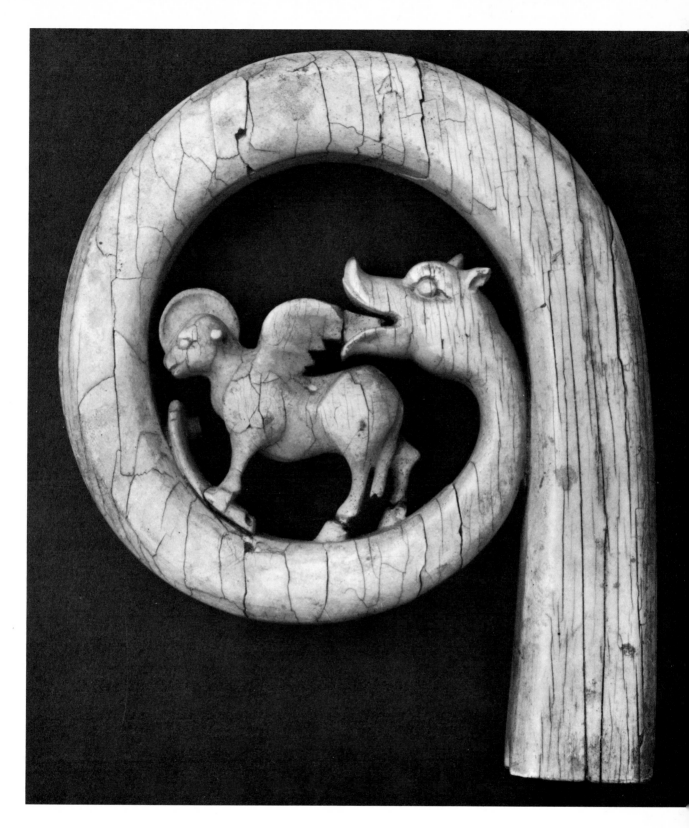

52 The pastoral crook, carried by bishops and also by the Egyptian Pharaohs (pl. 13), is a symbol of divine creative power. That it is also the staff of the guide who leads the soul on its spiral journey of regeneration, is here symbolized by the rebirth of the lamb of God from the jaws of the serpent. Representing death and initiation, to be swallowed symbolizes the return to the preformal, the chaotic or unconscious. Rebirth, like emergence from the labyrinth, is the triumph of order and the achievement of mastery over the natural serpent forces. (Crozier, Italian, 12th century.)

53 The Irish monks, working on their rocky islands, were completely surrounded by the ocean—their constant reminder of the perpetual flow and vortical movement of the cosmos. This so-called 'ornamental page' of the Book of Durrow is a page for meditation and preparation for the truth of the gospels to follow. Made up of one line, like the folding and unfolding of the Islamic arabesque (see also pls. 42, 56, 58), these Celtic whorls represent the continuous creation and dissolution of the world. (Page from Book of Durrow, Ireland, 7th century.)

54 The continuity of the coiling and uncoiling of life is also the theme of the huge spirals found in Neolithic China, exclusively on funerary objects. Entering into this womb-shaped cavity, the spirit of the dead is put into contact with the cosmic forces of regeneration represented by the double spirals. Between two spirals, the opening of the womb symbolizes the division between life and death, death and rebirth. (Funerary urn, China, 2nd millennium BC.)

55,56 Entrance to the 'Holy of Holies'. Passing a spiral barrier into an inner sanctuary seems, like the passage through the labyrinth, to have been a necessary passport into the sacred realm. This realm of immortality is reached by a real or symbolic death from the relative and transient natural world, and rebirth into the land of the dead—or the next world. This theme is found throughout the Megalithic and Neolithic worlds: in much of Europe, in Mexico, in China and in Egypt. Such spirals demonstrate the evolutionary nature of the journey being made. Since very often there are two dominant spirals, like the eyes of Horus (pl. 13) or the spiral 'oculi' at the entrance to the Maltese temple of Al Tarxien (left), they suggest the balancing of the opposing vortical energies, by which the state of wholeness or enlightenment is reached. As in passing between the two opposing columns of the Tree of Life (figs. 20–30), the initiate or soul is put into contact with the vertical still axis, the unmoved mover around which the natural world revolves. (55 Temple of Al Tarxien, Malta, 2400–2300 BC; 56 Threshold stone at entrance to tumulus at New Grange, Ireland, 3rd or 4th millennium BC.)

57,58 Chinese legends tell of the 'animals in the mirror'. Mirror backs were used as mandalas, for meditation, and usually depicted the animals of the four directions. Here these animals are sub-servient to the symmetry of the six directions of space, seen as the cycles of time around the still centre. These cycles of the manifest universe are multiple reflections of the One. As the universe has been likened to a mirror in which God contemplates himself, so the mirror is for self-contemplation. Like the reflecting moon (pl. 45), it is the door through which the soul may pass. The union of heaven, man and earth is represented here by its predominant

threefold arrangement; as in the three balls on the finial on top of the Islamic dome, this is the primordial involutionary vortex into matter. Traditionally nomadic, the Moslem expresses his eternal pilgrimage through the world in the arabesque which rolls and unrolls in a continuous thread like the breath of the cosmos; as it contracts and expands, it creates the very universe itself. This cupola of heaven is the divine heart which encloses all creation. (57 Bronze mirror-back, China, 4th-3rd century BC; 58 The Madraseh-yi-Madar-I-Shah, Isfahan, Iran, 1706–14.)

59 Fertility, through cosmic harmony, is achieved by the dance
in which the young virgins of the Bavenda tribe identify with the
serpent force. After the rains, during these ceremonial days, the
old women initiate the virgins, conduct the ceremony, and act as
the pivot around which the dancers spiral in the rhythmic movements and sinuous coils of the python. Collapsing and reviving,
they rest like the forces of nature in the seasonal round of death
and rebirth. (Deumba or python dance of the Bavenda, South
Africa.)

60 Embodying the celestial movements of a planet around its own axis and around the sun, the Dervish, by his whirling, realizes the spiralling of the universe into being. The contraction of spirit into matter takes place around the still axis of his own heart. His right (active) hand receives the manifestation of the One and his left turns it into the earth; his spirit, like the alternate breath of the cosmos, milled free of its illusory existence, expands and spirals to its Divine source. (The Order of the Mevlevi, the Dervish Dancers, Konya, Turkey.)

61 Sri Yantra depicting the creation. From the marriage between the central point (the original non-manifest seed Bindu), which is the pure consciousness of Siva, and his own first manifestation as the initial involutionary and creative vortex of the female Sakti (the downward triangle), comes the differentiation of the entire manifest world. The multiplicity of this world is shown by the interpenetration of the upward male triangles and the downward female triangles: the ascending and descending vortices of creative energy. The world's uncoiling is shown by the lotus-petals around the edge unfolding through the four directions of space or four gates. Just as creation is the ordering of chaos, mandalas which represent this creation (seen as a simultaneous rather than a linear time process) are diagrams which order and integrate the mind. (Sri Yantra, rock crystal, Nepal, ?17th century.)

62 The cosmic mandala from Bhutan is one of a series on a temple wall which describe successively the spiral involution of energy into matter. This enormous fresco is the depiction by an old lama of the 'Mystic Spiral', the primary movement of the universe. Spinning in the centre is the triple spiral; Like the downward vortex-triangle of the Sri Yantra, this is the first creative movement of the universe, which in later frescoes turns into the unfolding four-fold swastika. Around this are the rings of future materializations; next are shown twelve geometrical solids (three for each element), and around these, floating on the blue clouds of ether, are twelve circles: two for each of the six directions, signified by their colour, and spiralling in such a way as to indicate the three dimensionality of this spherical mandala. (The Mystic Spiral. mandala fresco, temple court of the fortress of Paro Dzong, West Bhutan.)

63,64 In his perpetual lunar calendar, showing the phases of the moon, Kircher has illustrated the unity of mathematics, mysticism and mythology. By using the growth properties of the arithmetical spiral, he has apparently indicated the lunar increments and the approximate dislocations in the daily time of moonrise. This makes it possible to read the hour of moonrise in each successive phase. The two right-handed spirals, representing the waxing and waning moons, are mirror images of each other; *Luna Crescens* expanding from the centre and *Luna Decrescens* contracting towards it. Since traditionally the spiral is associated and even identified with the moon (see pls. 44, 45), by relating the lunar phases to the solar phases or days, Kircher has, like the present day artist Vardanega, related the circle and the spiral, the male and the female. Vardanega has described his work as the using of 'circular structures in asymmetrical displacement *ad infinitum*'. (63 The Phases of the Moon, by Athanasius Kircher, Germany, 17th century; 64 Development of a circle to infinity, by Gregorio Vardanega, France, 1962.)

65 The Golden Egg of Brahma appears again at the beginning of every new cycle. 'This [Universe] existed in the shape of darkness, unperceived, unattainable by reasoning, unknowable, wholly immersed, as it were, in a deep sleep. Then the divine self . . . appeared with irresistable creative power, dispelling the darkness. He who is subtle, indiscernable and eternal, who contains all created beings and is inconceivable, shone forth. When the divine one wakes, then this world stirs, when he slumbers tranquilly, the universe sinks into sleep. Thus he, the imperishable one alternately waking and slumbering, incessantly revivifies and destroys the whole of creation.' (*The Laws of Manu.*) (Hiranyagarbha, tempera painting, India, *c.* 1775–1800.)

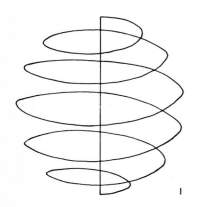

1

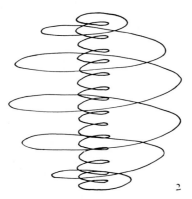

2

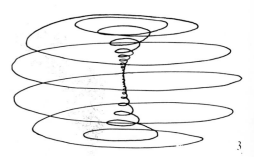

3

Documentary illustrations
and commentaries

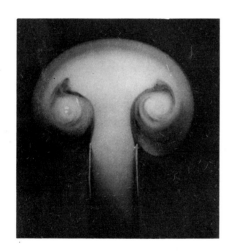

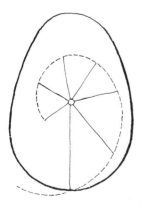

5

The awakening cosmos

The first vibrations of the egg of the world, which unfold to the confines of the universe (5), are seen by the author (1–3, far left) as both expanding and contracting, emerging from the source and going on to disappear into it, on a *spherical vortex*.

1–3 The still centre is the axis creating subject and object: the axis of consciousness (1). The universal continuum is shown perpetually spinning through its own centre (2, 3).
4 A vortex ring forms like many things in nature. This coloured liquid streaming into still water will become independent and spin vertically through its own centre.
5 The world egg as seen by the Dogon of West Africa.

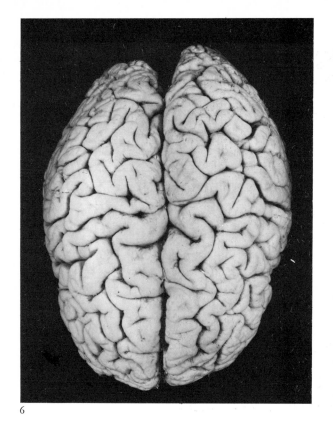

6

9

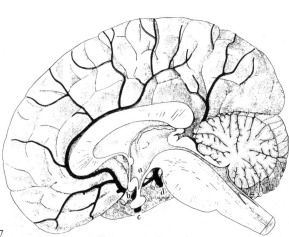

7

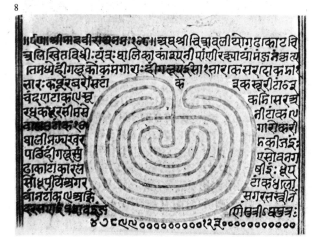

8

The labyrinth of the mind

The head is the inner sanctuary of the temple of man's body, both created and protected by the windings of the labyrinth. With each turn man completes a stage in his evolution. In the centre of the spiral he meets himself (11); this is his higher or complete Self, symbolized by Christ (12). The overall form of the brain, like the invaginating embryo, like the kidney or the archetypal growth form of the mushroom, resembles the natural form of flow (4).

6, 7 The number of *gyri* (windings) or folds of the cerebral cortex (7) is greater in man than in any other creature, since an increased surface area is necessary for higher mental processes. (Dorsal view of the human brain; cross-section of the human brain, courtesy *Scientific American*, January 1961.)

8 In the Indian tradition both the natural form of the brain (6, 7) and the 8-fold stages of the mind (*manas*) are identified with the form and windings of the labyrinth. (Manas-Chakra, Rajasthan, 18th century.)

9 The entrail demon Humbaba is the windings of the underworld which the hero enters, and the king of the underworld whom the hero slays. 'I have a long journey to go', says Gilgamesh, 'to the land of Humbaba. I must travel an unknown road and fight a strange battle.' Humbaba, whose 'jaws are death itself', guards the great maze-forest with his 7-fold terrors. With the exception of the eyes, this mask is made up of a single winding. (Mask of Humbaba, terracotta, Babylonian, early 2nd millennium BC.)

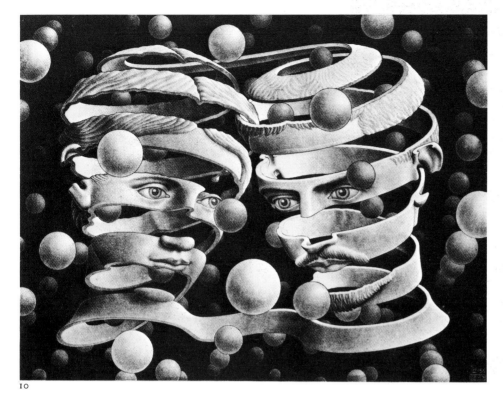

10

11

At the centre of the spiral labyrinth, man meets, overcomes, and thus unites with, Humbaba or the Minotaur, the 'monster' of his own hidden nature, and is reborn into a new state of wholeness. The centre is thus a symbol for the state of balance, of no-time or infinity (see 57, 58 and pl. 24).

10 Escher has shown this infinity as the balancing of opposites, with male and female as a continuum of two intertwined spherical vortices. (Band-Bond of union, lithograph by M. C. Escher, 1956.)
11 Labyrinth with oculiform face in the centre. (Rock engraving, Camonica Valley, Italy, 3rd–2nd millennium BC, from E. Ananti, *Camonica Valley*, Cape, London 1964.)
12 Labyrinth-mandala with head of Christ at the centre. (Page from psalter, Marienthal, near Zittau, Germany, 13th century.)

12

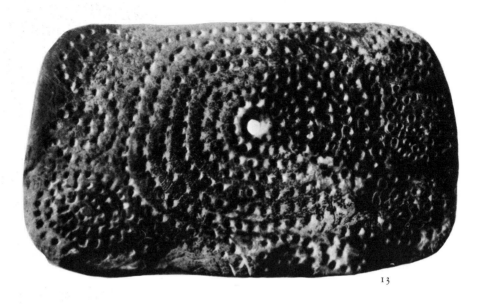

13

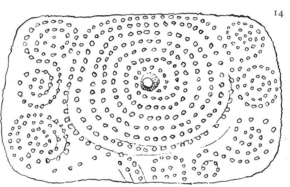

14

15

16

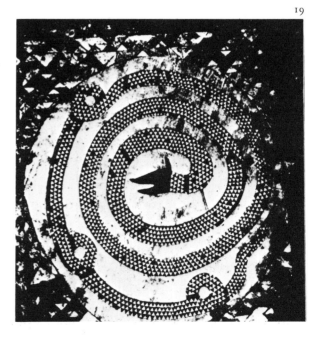

Serpent Mandalas

Mandalas, or diagrams which create order within man like the labyrinth, often show the 'serpent force' of his subtle body. Once flowing, this energy may bring enlightenment and a state of wholeness: the balance in the still centre of the spiral. This experience of timelessness, is the infinity symbolized by the serpent, which by sloughing its skin is continuously dying and being reborn. In all except the first of these mandalas, the serpent or spiral has $3\frac{1}{2}$ windings, like the inner serpent Kundalini (20, 22, 23).

13, 14 The first spiral known in the history of art, a Palaeolithic talisman from a ritual cave burial in Siberia, shows a 7-fold (twice $3\frac{1}{2}$) spiral surrounded by four double spirals, and backed by three wavy serpents. (Talisman, mammoth ivory, Mal'ta, Lake Baikal region, Siberia.)
15, 16 European mandalas made by two of Jung's patients during the course of individuation. The process of development proves on closer inspection, wrote Jung, 'to be cycladic or spiral . . . we can hardly help feeling that the unconscious moves spiralwise around a centre gradually getting closer, while the characteristics of the centre grow more and more distinct'. In 15, the centre shows the fourfold aspect of wholeness; in 16, the centre is the egg, which, like the hole at the centre of the Palaeolithic ivory, encompasses all. (Mandalas by women patients of C. G. Jung, from *Archetypes and the Collective Unconscious*, Routledge, London 1969.)
17 The Mexican feathered serpent shows the union of heaven (bird) and earth (snake).
18 A spiral labyrinth with $3\frac{1}{2}$ central windings, known as the 'Shepherd's Race', formerly at Boughton Green, Northants. (After Trollope's Memoir, 1858.)
19 Italian church pavement; snake-labyrinth. (Mosaic, Curia, formerly S. Adriano, Rome, 6th–12th c.)

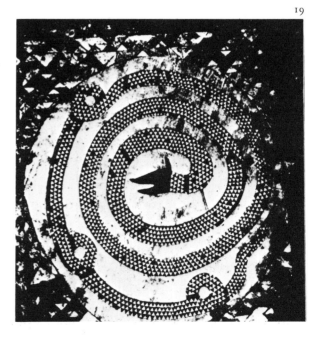

Man's secret body: tree and temple

The coilings of the serpent force within the subtle body: the Indian Kundalini and Cabbalistic Serpent of Wisdom.

20 The opposing solar and lunar energy channels, Pingala and Ida, spiralling round the neutral Sushumna and the seven chakras. (Lama Govinda, *The Foundations of Tibetan Mysticism*, Rider, London 1960.)

21 The serpent of wisdom, drawn by Aleister Crowley, spiralling up through the paths (mostly omitted) and Sephiroth of the Tree of Life (see 40, 41).

22 Kundalini asleep at the base of the Sushumna. (Scroll painting, Rajasthan, *c.* 18th century.)

23 Kundalini. (Anatomical drawing, India, 1st century AD.)

20

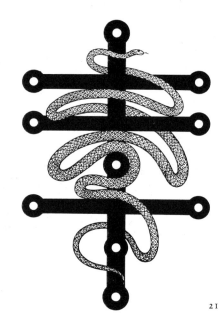

21

22

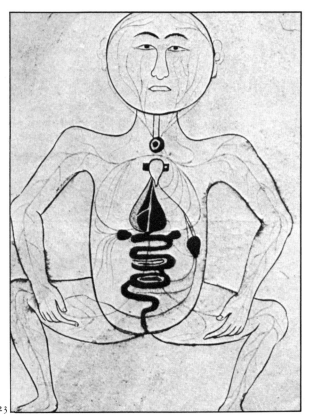

23

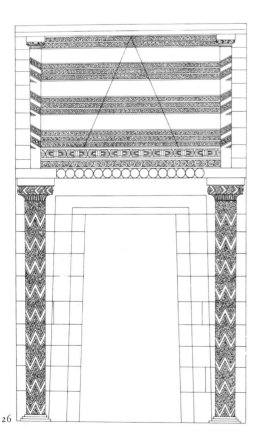

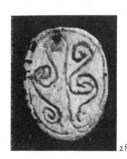

By passing over the threshold, between the opposing pillars of the Tree of Life, or by balancing his vortical energy centres, man himself becomes the still centre, the axis of equilibrium (see 30). This represents – either literally or through initiation – death and rebirth into the new world beyond.

24 One of the 4-directional gates (now damaged) around the central Great Stupa of Sanchi. (India, 1st century BC.)
25 Ionic columns. (Temple of the Erechtheum, Acropolis, Athens, late 5th century BC.)
26, 27 The Treasury of Atreus, royal tomb at Mycenae, diagram and pillar detail. (Green marble, c. 1125 BC, British Museum, London.)
28 Vortical energy centres symbolized on an early Egyptian scarab (see pl. 43). (Seal, steatite, possibly local copy, Lebanon, early 2nd millennium BC, Department of Antiquities, Beirut.)

The earth's body: temple and cave

Initiation is death from one state and rebirth into another; thus entering the labyrinth or the underworld is returning to the womb of the Earth Mother for a new birth.

29

29 The great megalithic Maltese temples were built in the form of the body of the Great Goddess. (Model of the temple of Ggantija, Gozo, 3rd millennium BC.)

30 Between man and this inner sanctuary, and guarding the threshold like the opposing pillars of the Tree of Life (24–27, 40), are the two oculi or womb spirals (see pls. 55, 56). (Temple of Al Tarxien, Malta, 2400–2300 BC.)

30

31

32

31 The warrior or initiate is seen fighting the oculiform face (11) at the centre of the labyrinth; the moment of death at the centre is followed by rebirth. (Rock engraving, Camonica valley, Italy, 3rd–2nd millennium BC, from E. Ananti, *Camonica Valley*, Cape, London 1964.)

32 This Toltec initiate, after being purified by burning water (bottom right), has to pass through the vortices of speech, the

Word of the gods (the scroll-like forms through which the path runs), before he can return to the seven caves of the original home of the race, to be reborn. (After Seler.)

33 On his night voyage through the underworld towards rebirth, the 'dead sun' is protected by the spiral coils of the serpent Mehen. (Tomb of Sety I, Valley of the Kings, West Thebes, Egypt, second millennium BC.)

33

Death and the balancing of worlds

The cross is man's body in a state of balance. At the point of
death he is balanced between two worlds. The spiral so often
depicted on funerary figures, stones and urns is the key which
opens the door into the next world. It is the spiral clue, the clew
or ball of thread that guides him through the labyrinth (seen on
the ancient Danish cross, 37).

34 Christ has at his navel the spiral by which he materialized
into this world. As he ascends, he will pass over the threshold
delineated by speech forms (see 32), the two winds or the sun
and moon. (Miniature from exultet roll, Rome, 12th century.)

35 The god is reborn from the jaws of the earth monster. In the
Cabbalistic Tree of Life, when there is an exchange between two
worlds, the point of knowledge (Daat) of one world becomes
the foundation (Yesod) of the world above; so in the body of
man, the third eye of one world becomes the navel of the next.
(Stela, Cozumalhuapa, Guatemala, 5th–9th century, Museum
für Völkerkunde, Berlin.)

36 The bishop (like Mercury, who carries the caduceus, pl. 11),
is the soul's guide; he carries his staff (pl. 52), which leads man
on his spiral journey. (Gravestone of Archbishop Ludolph,
Magdeburg Cathedral, 1192.)

35

34

36

37 The labyrinth is found at all times and places. In Christendom it appears not only on the pavement floors of many medieval cathedrals, but also on ancient stone crosses. (Danish runic cross, after O. Worm, *Antiquitates Danicae* 1651.)

38 A Greek tombstone showing the soul on its journey, shining with radiant light. In the crown of flames is the pearl and symbol of perfection (see pl. 19). (Archaeological Museum, Athens.)

39 This cross (like the more anthropomorphic Athlone Crucifix, pl. 15) shows the vortices at the heart of man's subtle body. On the right are the intertwined dragons, the balanced energies signified by the caduceus. The seven spirals, like the windings at the centre of pl. 42, show the six directions of space and the still centre. Around these are the four spheres or worlds, and at the head is the diagonal cross: the ascending and descending vortices. (Parish cross, Aberlemno, Scotland.)

38

39

37

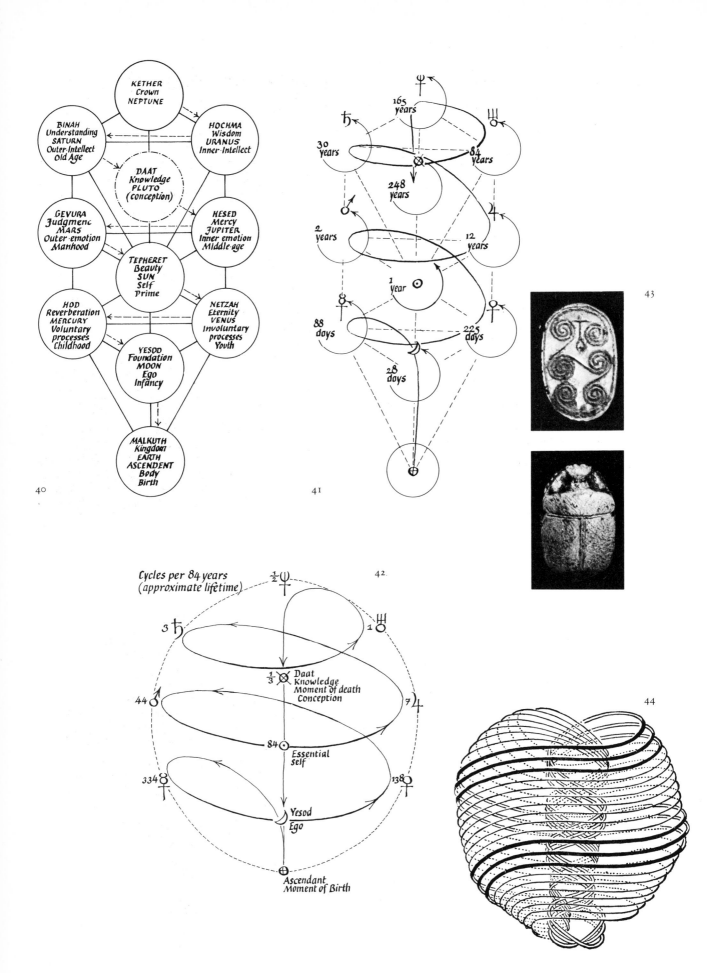

40

KETHER
Crown
NEPTUNE

BINAH
Understanding
SATURN
Outer-Intellect
Old Age

HOCHMA
Wisdom
URANUS
Inner-Intellect

DAAT
Knowledge
PLUTO
(conception)

GEVURA
Judgment
MARS
Outer-emotion
Manhood

HESED
Mercy
JUPITER
Inner-emotion
Middle-age

TEPHERET
Beauty
SUN
Self
Prime

HOD
Reverberation
MERCURY
Voluntary
processes
Childhood

NETZAH
Eternity
VENUS
Involuntary
processes
Youth

YESOD
Foundation
MOON
Ego
Infancy

MALKUTH
Kingdom
EARTH
ASCENDENT
Body
Birth

41

165 years
30 years
84 years
248 years
2 years
12 years
1 year
88 days
225 days
28 days

42

Cycles per 84 years
(approximate lifetime)

½ ♆
1 ♅
3 ♄
⅓ ⊗ Daat
Knowledge
Moment of death
Conception
44 ♂
7 ♃
84 ⊙ Essential
self
334 ☿
138 ♀
Yesod
Ego
Ascendant
Moment of birth

43

44

108

The Tree of Life and the heart

40 The Tree of Life (see pp. 22–24), showing the Sephiroth; some human and planetary correspondences; the passive (left), neutral (centre) and active (right) pillars. The descent of light from above (the lightning flash) is the path of the original creation, the bringing of heaven down to earth.

41 Man returns along the same path and dissolves the original creation. Taking earth back to heaven, he travels through all the planetary spheres. The orbit-times of these take gradually longer, like the development of their corresponding faculties within man.

42 The Tree of Life and the life-cycle seen as a spherical vortex (see p. 8), a rounded entity which expands from, contracts and returns on to its source.

43 An Egyptian scarab (initiate, see pl. 43) showing the vortical movement within the energy centres and the relationships between them (see also pls. 15, 28). (Seal, possibly local copy, Lebanon, early 2nd millennium BC, Beirut, Department of Antiquities.)

44 A clairvoyant's picture of the heart of the universe; the ultimate physical atom seen as a manifestation of pure light force spinning perpetually through itself. (C. W. Leadbeater, *The Chakras*, Theosophical Publishing House, Madras 1971.)

45 The human heart, showing the muscles and their spiral fibres which contract to twist the blood from its cavities. (*Scientific American*, May 1957.)

46 The Islamic prayer niche or *mihrab* has been called a reminder of the Divine presence in the heart. Leading off the dome, the all-encompassing heart of heaven, the *mihrab* is the inner sanctuary where the word of God is sounded. Spiralling throughout this niche and through the shell of the divine ear, are the vortices of the reverberating Word. (Mausoleum of Shaykh Muhammad ibn Bakran, Pir Bahran, Iran, 1299–1312.)

47 A mandala mirror-back from Iron-Age Britain. Reflecting the multiple images of the One, the mirror is an instrument of meditation (pl. 57). Like the configurations in the flow of water, these continuous windings transform into all kinds of natural forms. (Desborough mirror, bronze, Britain, 1st century AD, British Museum, London.)

46

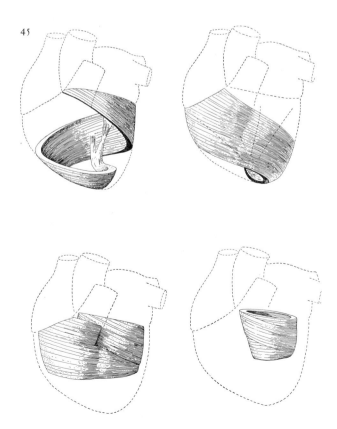

45

47

48

50

49

Mazes

The labyrinth both creates and protects the centre, and allows entry only on the correct terms. Entry is thus initiation, a step on the path of knowledge. But before knowledge is revealed, the old preconceptions must be dissolved by re-entry into the preformal state of the womb. The pot (48, 49) is a symbol of the body and womb of the Mother, and in Neolithic Europe it was often marked with the windings of the underworld.

48 Pithos from Pseira. (Archaeological Museum, Heraklion, Crete.)
49 Clay pot from Vadastra. (Romania, *c.* 3500–2700 BC, Bucharest Historical Museum.)
50 The Zulus draw mazes in the sand with their fingers. This one, drawn after smoking hemp, is like a game. 'You are done for in the labyrinth' they shout, when someone fails to reach the centre, the 'royal hut'. (L. H. Samuelson, *Some Zulu Customs and Folklore*, London 1928.)

51

52

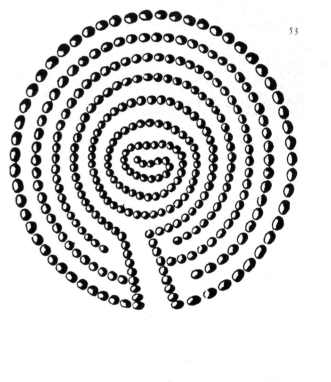

53

51 The Hopi Indians call the labyrinth the 'Mother Earth' symbol, and liken it to their own underground sanctuaries, the Kivas. It was from here that the Hopi emerged from the preceding world. 'All the lines and passages within the maze form the universal plan of the Creator, which man must follow on his Road of Life.' (Drawing by Oswald White Bear Fredericks, © 1963 by Frank Waters, from Frank Waters, *The Book of the Hopi*, Viking Press, New York 1969.)

52 A coin from Knossos, home of the 'original' labyrinth. The pastoral crook and the Yin Yang symbol can both be found amongst its windings. (Tetradrachm, Knossos, 1st millennium BC, British Museum, London.)

53 Labyrinth of large pebbles found in 1838 by Dr von Baer, on the uninhabited Island of Wier. (Finland.)

54 Labyrinth scratched on a painted pillar 2000 years ago, in the house of Lucretius, with the observation: *Labyrinthus, hic habitat Minotaurus.* (Pompeii, before AD 79.)

54

55

56

57

58

59

The warrior

'If your friend were a warrior . . . he would stop the world.'
(Don Juan, in Carlos Castaneda, *Journey to Ixtlan*, 1973.)

Time is verticalized in this moment of conquest. The hero has
realized the still centre of the labyrinth; only the winds sustain
him, lend power to his lance, and spiral in cosmic affirmation.
'I discovered the forest; its length is ten thousand leagues in
every direction. Enil has appointed Humbaba to guard it. What
man would willingly walk into that country and explore its
depths?' The God Shamash 'appointed strong allies for Gilgamesh . . . and stationed them in the mountain caves. The
great winds he appointed: the north wind, the whirlwind, the
storm and the icy wind . . .' (*The Epic of Gilgamesh*, tr. N. K.
Sandars, Penguin, London 1960.)

55 Grave stele. (Shaft grave V, Mycenae, *c.* 2000–1550 BC,
Mycenae, National Museum, Athens.)
56 Between the warriors and their horses is a fourfold spiralling
mandala. Like the Sri Yantra (pl. 61), it has four gates or directions, as well as differentiating into nine as a combination of four
and five. Each circle here has a different structure and mandalic
configuration. (Gotland stone, Vallstena, Sweden, 5th c. BC.)
57 St George. (Uccello, National Gallery, London; see pl. 24.)
58 'Theseus fights the Minotaur in the labyrinth', from a cosmographic MS. (Collected and transcribed at St Emmeram, post
1145, Bayerische Staatsbibliothek, Munich.)
59 The invincible Achilles, whose shield bore the protective
labyrinth, has his protection here in the spirals on his breast.
Shown here killing the Queen of the Amazons, Penthesilea, he
was the hero who gained entry and broke the defences of Troy
by dragging the body of Hector three times around its walls.
(Detail of neck-amphora by Exekias, Vulci, Italy, *c.* 530 BC.)
60 In the Indian epic *Mahabharata*, the warrior priest-magician
says: 'Today I will also form an array that is impenetrable to the
very gods.' This labyrinth, infused with special power, has the
king at its centre, and is created to keep out all but the chosen
victim: the youngest and purest of the enemy. As the young
boy's father had taught him how to enter but not how to escape
from the labyrinth, he is sacrificed at the centre. (Frieze,
Halebid, Mysore, India, 12th–13th century AD.)
61 A labyrinth ritual on an Etruscan wine-jar. The warriors are
seen emerging from the maze with its retroscript title: TRUIA.
Mentioned by Virgil, the Trojan Game (or maze dance) was a
secret even in antiquity; it was associated with the weaving of
powerful magical fields for initiatory rituals. (Tracing from the
Tragliatella Oinochoe, Rome, 7th century BC, from W. H.
Matthews, *Mazes and Labyrinths*, Dover, New York 1970.)

60

61

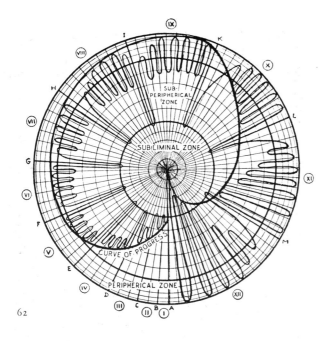

62

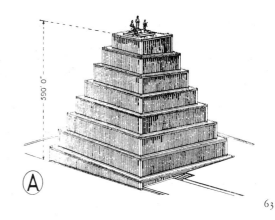

Ⓐ

63

65

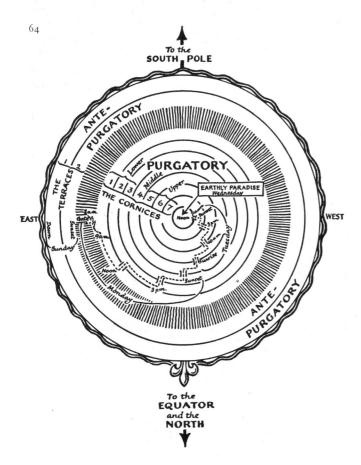

64

THE EARTHLY PARADISE			
UPPER PURGATORY	Excessive Love of Secondary Good	Disordered Love of Good	Cornice 7 – The Lustful
			Cornice 6 – The Gluttonous
			Cornice 5 – The Covetous
MIDDLE PURGA-TORY		Love Defective	Cornice 4 – The Slothful
LOWER PURGATORY	Love of Neighbours' harm. (Love Perverted)		Cornice 3 – The Wrathful
			Cornice 2 – The Envious
			Cornice 1 – The Proud
PETER'S GATE		Steps:	3. Satisfaction
			2. Contrition
			1. Confession
ANTE – PURGATORY	Salvation in articulo mortis	Terrace 2	The Late Repentant :– (a) The Indolent (b) The Unshriven (c) The Pre-occupied
		Terrace 1	The Excommunicate

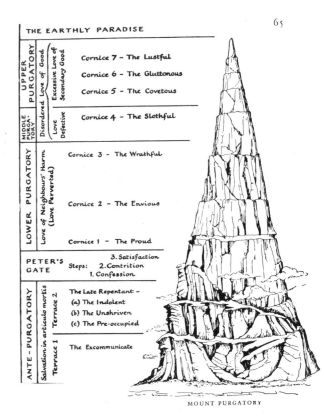

MOUNT PURGATORY

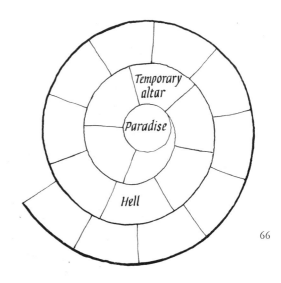

66

114

The structure and development of consciousness

62 Lama Govinda shows the development of consciousness as a double spiral. Moving outwards from the centre, from an original unconscious unity like that of the child, its development gets progressively differentiated towards the periphery, which represents the usual surface-consciousness and maximum of differentiation. This is the turning-point and the start of the inward spiral towards the centre, towards the *conscious* unity of the enlightened. (Figure from Lama Govinda, *The Psychological Attitude of Early Buddhist Philosophy*, Rider, London 1961.)

63–65 Diagram 62 may also be imagined in three dimensions, as a cone, just as 64 is the plan of Dante's Mount Purgatory, the mountain journey of 65. The ascent of the 'holy mountain', like the temple or the ziggurat (63), represents the spiral development of consciousness. That which is disordered and differentiated at the base or periphery becomes concentrated and ordered at the point or centre. The ziggurat, according to ancient Babylonian tradition, had seven windings for the seven planets or celestial orbits. (Chaldaean single ramp temple, from Banister Fletcher's *A History of Architecture*, Batsford, London 1924; plan and elevation of Mount Purgatory, from Dante's *Inferno*, tr. D. M. Sayers, Penguin, London 1961.)

66 Hopscotch is called in German *Tempel-* or *Himmelhüpfen* (temple or heaven hopping), and recalls the labyrinth ritual done by the children of ancient Tuscany and Rome (61). Children's games come from a common source and hold on to religious and mythic patterns long after these have become esoteric and disappeared from the general culture. The drawing shows an old French form of hopscotch, or *marelles*, called *la marelle ronde* or *le colimaçon* (the snail). It shows, like the mountain of Purgatory (65) or the ziggurat (63), the different stages on the mystic path.

67 The vajra, or 'diamond sceptre' in the Buddhist tradition, is the symbol of the highest spiritual power. It shows the original point, Bindu, containing its potential spiral unfolding (I). Although never moving from its central position, the point unfolds (II, III) and becomes the central axis – the polarity and union of opposites – surrounded by the lotus petals of the four directions. The spiral at the centre is both the original subjective knowledge and that gained by the balancing of opposites (of subject and object). The diamond sceptre (like fig. 62) thus shows the primordial unity of consciousness, its outward path to the periphery and its return to the centre. (Figure from Lama Govinda, *Foundations of Tibetan Mysticism*, Rider, London 1960.)

68 The jewel in this contemporary American postcard is shown with the same purging or clarifying power as the spirals of the Indian sceptre or the path up Mount Purgatory. Only the message is more direct.

69 While colourless, the diamond contains all colours; while it can cut anything, nothing can cut it. Consisting in the same atoms as coal or graphite, the diamond demonstrates the transformation of a substance from a state of disorder to one of supreme order and clarity.

68

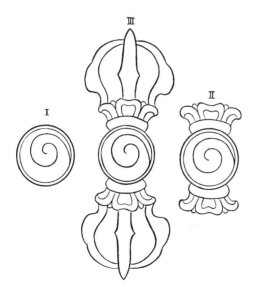

67

69

70

71

The split in the World Egg

'The divine one resided in that egg during a whole year, then he himself by his thought [alone] divided into two halves, and out of these two halves he formed heaven and earth.' (*The Laws of Manu.*) The double spiral shows the two halves of the spherical vortex, or of Plato's 'androgynous spherical man'; it is both primordial and final, both seed and goal. The double spiral shows the continuity between polarities and is the alternate involution and evolution, rolling and unrolling, of the cosmos: its in- and outbreath, contraction and expansion. In Taoism the double spiral (Yin and Yang) is the alternate condensation and dissipation; in alchemy it is coagulation and solution. It is the opposing energy currents within the body of man. Macrocosmically it is the days and nights of Brahma; individually it is man's birth and death.

70 This ancient fibula or brooch is one continuous bronze wire. 'The whole is, so to speak, a puzzle: for what one sees when the device is in act, is only the two spirals, and it is not apparent that the whole is really an endless circle in which the visible spirals are the knots: we do not "see the point". The last end and the first beginning coincide.' (A. K. Coomeraswamy.) (Bronze wire fibula, Greece, 10th century BC, Metropolitan Museum of Art, New York, Fletcher Fund, 1937.)

71 The Hopi migration symbol. From their point of emergence to the fourth world, the Hopi clans made a four-directional spiral migration throughout the whole of America, as a purification and weeding-out of the evil brought from the previous world. These signs on rocks, pottery and altar boards show the patterns made by the individual clans as they spiralled in again upon their centre to be reunited at their permanent home. (Drawing by Oswald White Bear Fredericks, © 1963 by Frank Waters, from Frank Waters, *The Book of the Hopi*, Viking Press, New York 1969.)

72, 73 Egyptian scarabs showing the double spiral. (Seals, quartz and steatite, possibly local copies, Lebanon, early 2nd millennium BC, Department of Antiquities, Beirut.)

74 The Dharma Wheel, symbol of the doctrines of Buddha or the Universal Law. The key to liberation, it shows the dynamic balancing of the threefold spiral: positive, negative and equilibrium. (Figure from John Blofeld, *The Way of Power*, Allen & Unwin, London 1970.)

75 The human soul to the Japanese is three interlocking spirals. Each of these *maga-tama* shows the fundamental structure of creation. (Painting by Eikei Kano, Katsura Imperial Palace, Kyoto, Japan; from *Splendours of the East*, © Weidenfeld & Nicolson, London 1965.)

76 The Yin Yang symbol is itself the third principle, that of equilibrium, formed by the dynamic balance of the opposing twofold principles. It is surrounded by the eight trigrams, like the eight spokes of the Dharma Wheel. (Wooden plate, Vietnam, 19th century, Musée de l'Homme, Paris.)

77 The balanced threefold spirals in the window of a medieval Cistercian abbey. (Val Meriel, Seine-et-Oise, France.)

72

73

74

75

76

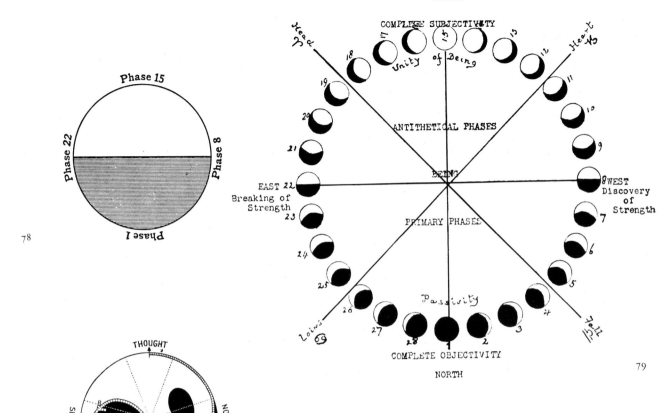

Phase 15

Phase 22 · Phase 8

Phase 1

78

SOUTH

COMPLETE SUBJECTIVITY

Unity of Being

ANTITHETICAL PHASES

BEING

PRIMARY PHASES

Head · Heart

EAST 22
Breaking of
Strength

WEST
Discovery
of
Strength

Passivity

Loins · Fall

COMPLETE OBJECTIVITY

NORTH

79

THOUGHT

SENSATION · INTUITION

FEELING

DIAGRAM V

80

81

Union of heaven and earth: dynamic equilibrium

The earth's horizon divides our consciousness (the celestial sphere) into what we can see (the light and our conscious) and what is obscured by the earth (the dark and our unconscious). The completed sphere is our source and goal; the model of our fully realized consciousness. Until this still point is reached, everything is cyclic movement around this sphere, between its polarities (the spiral of the spherical vortex).

78 Yeats' diagram shows these two halves in a static relationship, while the Chinese Ying Yang (80) shows them in dynamic equilibrium. (W. B. Yeats, *A Vision*, Macmillan, London 1937.)

79 Yeats' diagram showing 28 stages between the polarities, in a complete cycle, visualized as the phases of the moon between no moon, full moon and no moon. While corresponding astrologically to the natal moon phase (the threefold angle between man, his sun or higher self and his moon, or ego), this cycle is that of *any* whole: 'every complicated movement of thought or life, twenty-eight incarnations, a single incarnation, a single judgment or act of thought'. (W. B. Yeats, *A Vision*, Macmillan, London 1937.)

80 What Blake calls the 'Four mighty ones . . . in every Man; a Perfect Unity', the 'Four Zoas' (85), seen on the Yin Yang symbol; only by a dynamic balance of his constituent parts can man complete the spiral development of his consciousness, from the still point of primal unity to that of the goal. Blake calls these 'the Four Faces of Humanity, fronting the Four Cardinal Points of Heaven, going forward, forward irresistible from Eternity to Eternity' (*Jerusalem*). These four are the first permutation of the polarity, and may be understood in terms of an astrological chart. This chart, a twelvefold circle, containing the planetary bodies in their natal constellations, is a plan of the celestial sphere of each person's consciousness. If there is a strong emphasis of planetary bodies above the horizon, then the person may be constitutionally extraverted; when this emphasis is

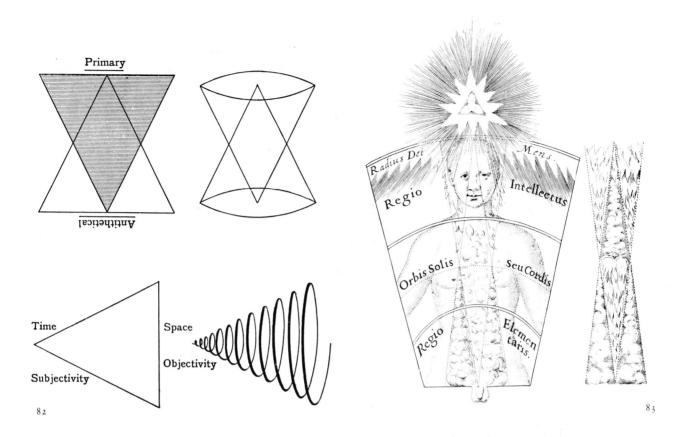

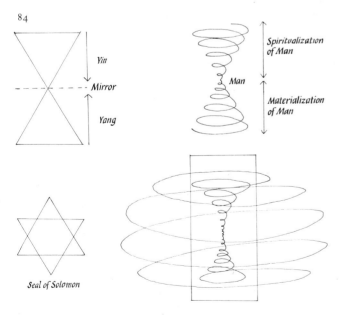

below, then there is a tendency towards introversion. These terms are Jung's primary twofold division of the psyche, and include the (internal) subjectivism, the direct response of *intuition*, and the (external) objectivism, the direct response of *sensation*. The celestial sphere is further divided by a vertical axis joining Midheaven to the Nadir. This is the 'now' of concrete experience which cuts through, reflects or measures these primary responses and gives rise to the secondary inner faculty of *feeling* and the secondary outer faculty of *thought*. (Figure from J. Jacobi, *The Psychology of C. G. Jung*, Routledge, London 1942.)

81 The complete cycle from the Chinese *I Ching*, showing 64 stages and thus a more complex permutation of the polarities, Yin and Yang (in combinations of 6). (The circular sequence according to Shao Yung, from H. Wilhelm, *Change*, Routledge, London 1961.)

82 Each of Yeats' gyres is a complete lunar cycle. Macrocosmically this is the great year which turns into its opposite every 2,000 years. Two opposing gyres, intersecting and whirling in opposite directions through the body, form the basis of his meditation and of the philosophical system of *A Vision*. In this he says: 'Line and plane are combined in a gyre which must expand or contract according to whether mind grows in objectivity or subjectivity.' (W. B. Yeats, *A Vision*, Macmillan, London 1937.)

83 The balanced, intersecting gyres (as triangles) centred on the heart, form the Perfect Man. (Robert Fludd, *Utriusque cosmi . . . historia*, II, 1619.)

84 Man's role is to connect and balance heaven and earth. The descending gyre of heaven is the materialization of spirit into matter, 'naming the Limit of Contraction Adam' (Blake, *Jerusalem*, 73). The ascending spiral is man's return path, his expansion into spirit and the dissolution of the original coils of manifestation. Thus the intersecting of these two vortices within the body, symbolized by the Seal of Solomon, shows man in a state of balance and dynamic equilibrium.

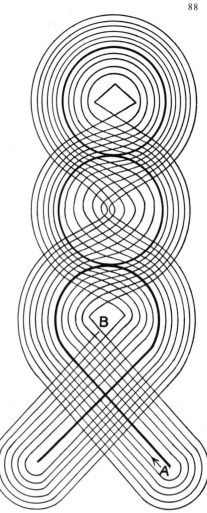

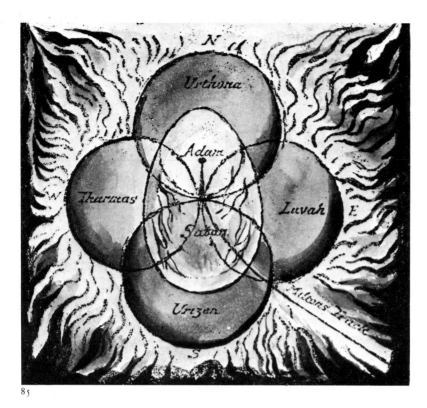

The Path

'Awake! awake, O sleeper of the land of shadows, wake! Expand!' (Blake, *Jerusalem*, 4.)

85 'And the Four Zoas clouded rage East & West & North & South; They changed their situations in the Universal Man . . . And the Four Zoas, who are the Four Eternal Senses of Man, Became Four Elements separating from the Limbs of Albion: These are their names in the Vegetative Generation' (*Jerusalem*, 36). Their four intersecting globes correspond to Jung's psychic functions (80); for Urthona is imagination, Urizon is reason, Tharmas is sensation and Luvah is feeling, together constituting the Giant Albion. Milton, one of the eternals, descends, like Jesus (90), as the saviour to our universe of Time, the Egg of Los situated within Albion, to show man the return path of self-annihilation. (Illustration by William Blake from 'Milton', 1804, British Museum, London.)

86 This labyrinth-mandala, from the tiles of an abbey, shows that, before man can reach the diamond body at the still centre of his being, he must know the way through each of his four parts. Like the traditional Eastern mandala, this is a circle, both eight- and sixteen-fold; it has four cardinal gates (between the beaks of the eight phoenixes) and contains a square. The square is delineated by a four-fold labyrinth, diagonally orientated as a cross; the vortices of heaven and earth meet at the centre. (Toussaints Abbey, Châlons-sur-Marne, France.)

87 Swastika-labyrinth showing the spiral 4-directional unfolding of space and time from the central star. (Tetradrachm from Knossos, 1st millennium BC, British Museum, London.)

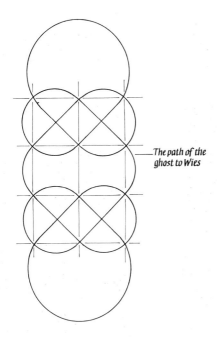

89

The path of the
ghost to Wies

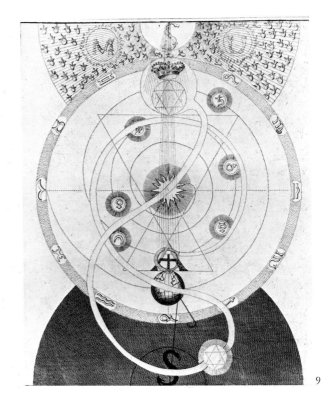

91

88, 89 After death, the ghost of the Malekulan journeys to Wies, Land of the Dead. Sitting on a rock and obstructing his way, is a guardian ghost. In the sand in front of her is a continuous line drawing. As soon as she sees him, she obliterates half of her maze and will devour his soul unless, remembering his ritual paths and the knowledge and wisdom of life, he can complete her line, the way of immortality. This continuous winding shows the three centres of man (like figs. 83, 92), his 'head, heart and guts', his thinking, feeling and moving 'brains', which Gurdjieff calls the 'bobbin kandlenosts' or spools. While their potential or length of thread is fixed, the key to the soul's life (three human lives) lies in their balanced unwinding. (Figure from *Folk-Lore*, XLVII, London 1936.)

90 Earth, K'un, receives into her the power of heaven, Ch'ien, the still centre manifest through the fourfold powers. Similar to Sakti in relation to Siva (p. 24), she unfolds in the four seasons and directions as the development of numbers, the odd (light and heavenly) and the even (dark and earthly), in the five states

of change. (The Yellow River Map of Fû Hsi, from C. G. Jung, *Collected Works*, IX, i, Routledge, London.)

91 The return spiral path shown to man by Christ. After descending at the Crucifixion to join with Adam, after spiralling back through the heavenly bodies as the Tree of Life in reverse of the original creation, Christ descends further to purify Hell, and then forms the ascending path for man to follow, to supreme union at the Crown. In the final perfection, the gyres (seen here as triangles beginning to penetrate) will interlock as the Seal of Solomon and union of heaven and earth. (Figure by William Law, from *The Works of Jacob Behmen* [Boehme], London 1763.)

92 Lama Govinda has shown the Buddhist eightfold path spiralling through the three bodies to the centre. The eight stages of the path are: right understanding, right intention, right speech, right action, right livelihood, right effort, right mindfulness and right absorption, or Samadhi. (Lama Govinda, *The Psychological Attitude of Early Buddhist Philosophy*, London 1961.)

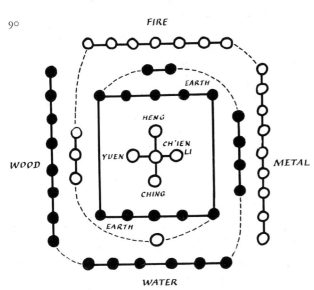

90

FIRE

EARTH

HENG

YUEN   CH'IEN
LI

CHING

WOOD

METAL

EARTH

WATER

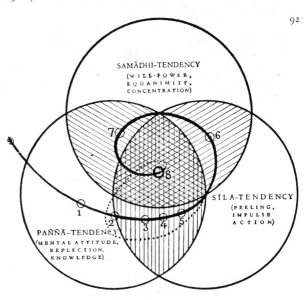

92

SAMĀDHI-TENDENCY
(WILL-POWER,
EQUANIMITY,
CONCENTRATION)

SĪLA-TENDENCY
(FEELING,
IMPULSE
ACTION)

PAÑÑĀ-TENDENCY
(MENTAL ATTITUDE,
REFLECTION,
KNOWLEDGE)

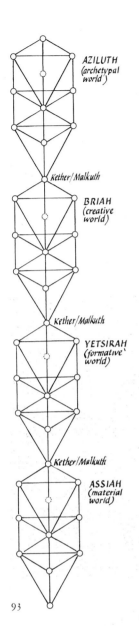

AZILUTH
(archetypal
world)

Kether/Malkuth

BRIAH
(creative
world)

Kether/Malkuth

YETSIRAH
(formative
world)

Kether/Malkuth

ASSIAH
(material
world)

93

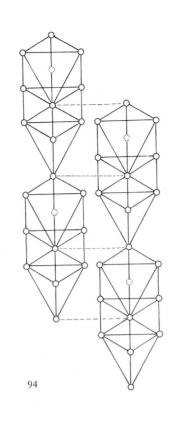

94

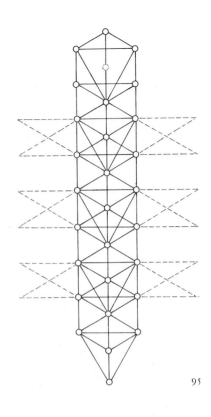

95

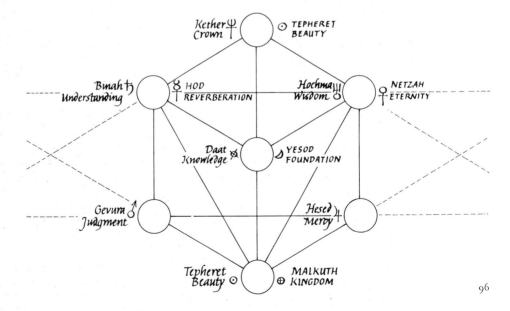

Kether Ψ
Crown ♀   ☉ TEPHERET
                    BEAUTY

Binah ♄   Hochma ♅
Understanding   ♀ HOD   Wisdom ☿   ♀ NETZAH
                 REVERBERATION   ETERNITY

        Daat ⊕   YESOD
     Knowledge   ☽ FOUNDATION

Gevura ♂   Hesed ♃
Judgment ♂   Mercy ♃

Tepheret ☉   MALKUTH
Beauty   ⊕ KINGDOM

96

Worlds, Dimensions and Directions

93-95 Creation in the Cabbala is seen as the vibratory extension of God himself in the form of four superimposed worlds. These are either implicit in a single Tree of Life, or seen as four Trees placed end to end (93), or in a third relationship, the four worlds are seen as interpenetrating (94, 95). Compare this with Blake's Four Zoas (85).

As the vibrations are more refined going up through the Trees, the dimensions increase. If our world has four dimensions, then the world above has five, and so on. As the dimension changes, so does the direction. If this world is predominantly right-handed or clockwise, then the world above is anticlockwise; thus it is traditionally thought possible to gain access to the next world through the mirror or the reflecting moon (see pls 44, 45).

96 When the successive worlds are seen as interlocking (94, 95), then between them is formed the Seal of Solomon, symbol of the interpenetrating vortices and union of worlds. The point at the centre of this figure is the Daat/Yesod exchange: the invisible knowledge of one world creating the foundation of the world above (see 103, p. 27).

97, 98 Ascending and descending spirals in nature. This geometric spiral of Wilcrick Hill, Monmouthshire, is winding upwards and to the left; the whirlpool spirals downwards and to the right. (Whirlpool from Theodor Schwenk, *Sensitive Chaos*, Rudolf Steiner Press, London 1971.)

99 A right- or a left-handed spiral traditionally indicates a choice between an upward and a downward path; although the direction here and in 97 and 98 is reversed. (Double spiral staircase carved out of the hill in the Vatican, Rome.)

97

98

99

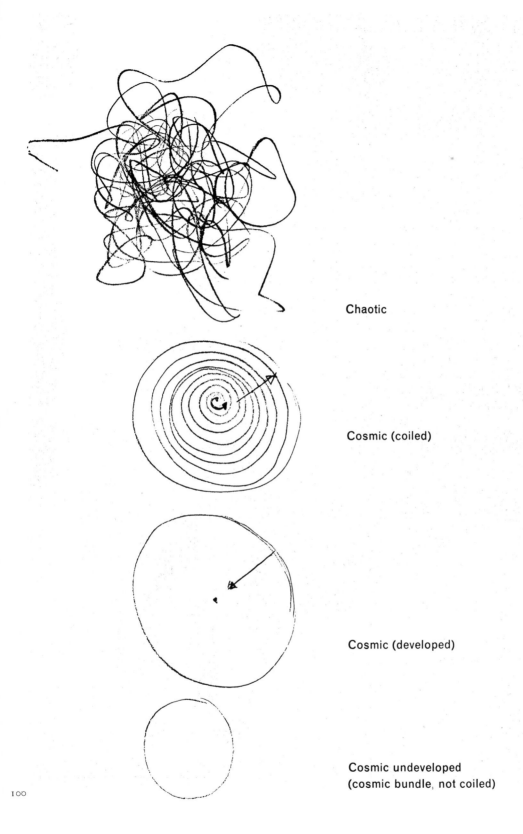

Chaotic

Cosmic (coiled)

Cosmic (developed)

Cosmic undeveloped
(cosmic bundle, not coiled)

Chaos – cosmos

100 From the notebooks of Paul Klee. (*The Thinking Eye*, Lund Humphries, London 1961.)

101

101 An infidel, a representative of chaos, is put into the service of cosmic order, the body of the cathedral. Order is reflected internally by the spiralling of the subtle energies within the body, here seen at the navel. (Pillar support, Ferrara Cathedral, Italy, *c.* 1140.)

102

103

104

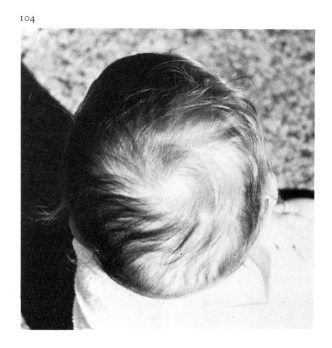

105

106

Cosmos and the dance of ecstasy

From macrocosm to man as microcosm. In the centre of any
spiral is the calm core through which man passes to eternity.

102 To a traveller through the universe, our own galaxy looks
like this; to us, looking through its spiral arm edgeways, it
appears as the Milky Way. (Whirlpool Nebula in *Canes
venatici*.)

103 'The city of Jericho was a similar shape to the moon', says
the author of this medieval manuscript. In the Cabbala, when
two worlds or Trees interlock, the position of Yesod (foundation, the moon) coincides with that of Daat (knowledge, Pluto;
see 94–96). To the ancients, the labyrinth was a part of founding
a town: cutting off a portion of space and transforming it from
chaos into cosmos. The windings which laid the foundation also
protected it from entry of all but those with knowledge, the
knowledge of the way. At the centre is a four-petalled flower.
(From cosmographic manuscript, collected and transcribed at
St Emmeram, post 1145, Bayerische Staatsbibliothek, Munich.)

104 The still point at the crown of the head. Shaved by monks,
this highest chakra is the Indian Thousand Petalled Lotus
through which cosmic light can enter the body.

105 A modern town being built in the form of a spiral. Auroville is the spiritual community founded by the Indian teacher
and revolutionary Aurobindo. (Model for Auroville, Pondi-
cherry, India.)

106 By dancing, by spinning around his own axis, in figures of
eight or around a sun, man incorporates the movements of the
universe, of planets and atoms, of galaxies and electrons. As he
winds, he creates the still point in his heart and turns the universe
into being; as he unwinds, he turns his spirit back to his divine
source. (Dore Hoyer, drawing by Johannes Richter, 1968.)

107 The humpbacked flute-player. (Emblem of Hopi flute clan,
drawing by Oswald White Bear Fredericks, © 1963 by Frank
Waters, from Frank Waters, *The Book of the Hopi*, Viking Press,
New York 1969.)

107

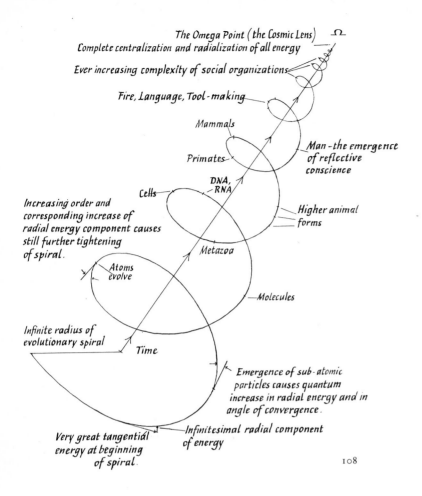

The Omega Point (the Cosmic Lens) Ω
Complete centralization and radialization of all energy

Ever increasing complexity of social organizations

Fire, Language, Tool-making

Mammals

Primates

Man - the emergence of reflective conscience

DNA, RNA

Cells

Increasing order and corresponding increase of radial energy component causes still further tightening of spiral.

Higher animal forms

Metazoa

Atoms evolve

Molecules

Infinite radius of evolutionary spiral

Time

Emergence of sub-atomic particles causes quantum increase in radial energy and in angle of convergence.

Very great tangential energy at beginning of spiral.

Infinitesimal radial component of energy

108

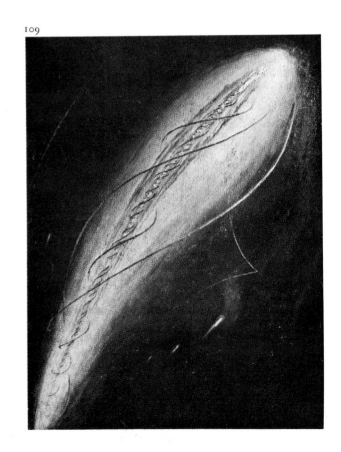

109

Evolution

108 The spiral of evolution according to Oliver Reiser.
109 The 'long body of the solar system' conceived in an eighty-year 'moment of perception', hurtling through the universe towards Vega at $12\frac{1}{2}$ miles a second. During this period, driven forward 30,000 million miles, 'The planetary paths, drawn out into manifold spirals of various tensions and diameters, have now become a series of iridescent sheaths veiling the long white-hot thread of the sun, each shimmering with its own characteristic colour and sheen, the whole meshed throughout by a goassamer-fine web woven from the eccentric paths of innumerable asteroids and comets, glowing with some sense of living warmth and ringing with an incredibly subtle and harmonious music.' (From Rodney Collin, *The Theory of Celestial Influence*, London 1954.)